WILL'S SHOOT

· REVISITED ·

Dedicated to all those who have helped over the
thirty-five years to make a dream
become a reality

WILL'S SHOOT
• REVISITED •

Will Garfit

Foreword by John Humphreys

• THE •
SPORTSMAN'S
PRESS

Copyright © 2005 William Garfit

First published in the UK in 1993
by The Sportsman's Press, an imprint of Quiller Publishing Ltd

This edition published 2005

The right of William Garfit to be identified as the author of this work has been asserted in accordance with the Copyright, Design and Patent Act 1988

British Library Cataloguing-in-Publication Data
A catalogue record for this book
is available from the British Library

ISBN 1 904057 61 6

Printed in China

The Sportsman's Press

An imprint of Quiller Publishing Ltd
Wykey House, Wykey, Shrewsbury, SY4 1JA
Tel: 01939 261616 Fax: 01939 261606
E-mail: info@quillerbooks.com
Website: www.swanhillbooks.com

CONTENTS

ACKNOWLEDGEMENTS

My thanks to gamekeepers, water bailiffs, wardens, foresters, nurserymen and naturalists and all from whom I have gleaned tips, shared from their overflowing country wisdom.

My thanks to Veronica for interpreting my handwriting and transposing it, via word processor, to 'disk', with patience, imagination and skill.

I would like to thank John Apthorp, owner of my original oil painting 'Evening flight at Hauxton', for permission for it to be reproduced on the cover of this book. He purchased this picture at an auction in aid of the Game Conservancy.

I would like to thank Michael Chinery for his list of butterflies. I am most grateful to Philip Oswald for coordinating his considerably extended botanical list with those of Ken Cramp, J. Jarvis, Jean Benfield and Graham Easy, and transposing them to conform with the B.S.B.I. list of English names as well as adding their scientific Latin names.

I would like to acknowledge Dave Parfitt for some of the black-and-white photographs used to illustrate the book.

My thanks to Sue Coley for her considerable help as editor of the book. She has maintained the flavour whilst sensitively and diplomatically steering the colloquial towards the literate.

The list of bird species recorded over the years is compiled from information supplied by Julian Limentani, Graham Easy, Stephen Percival and Roger Jeeves in addition to my own and I would like to thank them for their help and valuable contribution.

Finally I must thank Andrew Johnston and his team at Quiller Publishing for creating this opportunity to update and extend the original *Will's Shoot* that the story may live on: perhaps to inspire others with a modest few acres and be an interesting read for all.

FOREWORD

Drive too fast up the High Street towards the church and you miss it. Allow your eye to become distracted by an approaching lorry and before you know it the chance has gone and the hidden entrance to Paradise has slipped by unobserved. However, travel with the decorum that befits a residential road and you just might notice, on the right, a green mist of willows bursting into bud, ripples from a lake might wink at you through the hedge, a clump of firs hints at Scandinavian mystery and behind them a micro landscape of rushes and reeds, mixed trees and bushes.

Little did you know it but you had been within yards of a very special place. Those lucky enough to be invited to pass through the green gates, sufficiently high, secure and opaque to maintain the mystery, will find their lives never quite the same again, for they have been privileged to visit fairyland, a hall of magic mirrors, always a surprise round the next corner and a new conjuring trick of topography to startle and intrigue.

The pages which follow chart the history and development of what started as a series of collapsed gravel workings, a jungle-cloaked marsh which might have been lifted and transported straight from the Okeefenokee swamplands; indeed, one corner of it has been christened The Everglades.

When the Almighty had it to himself this scrap of real estate was nothing much, unprepossessing even, home to colonies of foxes, magpies, feral cats and rats. No doubt He was too preoccupied elsewhere to pay it much heed but the spark He needed to get it going was a chap as enterprising and imaginative as the author of this book. An impoverished art student at the time he found his hand shooting up at the auction and before he knew it Hauxton Pits were knocked down to him at rather more than he was prepared to pay; the delight of the new owner was tinged with alarm as he recalled the parlous state of his bank balance. What followed was to have repercussions on a whole generation of shooting conservationists up and down the land.

From the early days I was one of the lucky ones, invited to share the thinking and planning, conscious of the sacrifice of family time, the economies needed to support the next development but then to taste the fruits which followed. Bit by bit things happened; old workings were re-sculpted by bulldozer drivers who had in their veins the blood of artists. Islands and promontories appeared, a fishing lodge nestled in the trees and a rustic footbridge took you across a corner of the lake. One day there was a field where once there had been scrub and carr, little pools, marshy corners, new plantings of trees, water weeds and secret, meandering paths came in succession, each of my visits a chance to inspect and admire the realisation of yet another part of the dream.

In the wake of this remodelling, the birds, beasts, plants, fishes and insects followed. The song of new birds enriched the summer mornings, butterflies hitherto unseen danced and flickered; carp and trout cruised and rolled on the surface, wild strawberries peeped through the grasses, rabbits scuttled, snipe, woodcock and duck colonised.

In their turn came the humans to share, besport themselves, enjoy and harvest the surplus which a rich and well-managed new environment had produced. Trout men swished their lines across the pools as the sedges trickled off at last light; in the next lake the carp anglers sat hunched as patient as old herons under green umbrellas; on the heath a ping of an air rifle shot heralded a rabbit rolled over for the pot.

On winter shooting days pheasants, woodcock and wildfowl were driven from belt to belt, from spinney and over lake for, surrounded by industrial wasteland, major roads and the village High Street they had nowhere else to go. Mallard and geese dropped in in the gloaming and sometimes found a flight shooter awaiting them; wood pigeons streamed into the tall willows in spring.

As well as the sportsmen there came the helpers, those on whom the spell of Hauxton had worked, who wanted just to be involved, mow grass, manage fish, beat on shooting days, set rat traps and keep down the crows. Just to walk round the paths was cathartic, for that green iron door shut out, for a little while, the tribulations of the world outside.

Will Garfit, author of this book, created the place, his was the thinking, his the energy, leadership and inspiration which turned a sixty-nine acre (twenty-eight hectare) plot of waste land into a place of quality, deemed worthy to be included in Brian Martin's book *The Great Shoots* alongside vast and ancient shooting estates; good enough to win the prestigious Laurent Perrier Award for Wild Game Conservation, good enough to inspire others to attempt to go and create such a place of their own – and I should know for I was one of them.

What follows is the story so far, for the last chapter will never be written; there is ever more to do and fresh ideas to try. For many readers this is the nearest they may get to slipping through that Fort Knox gate in the High Street for many call but few are chosen. You might have to make do with the words and pictures that follow, but console yourself with the thought that you will put down this book at the end certainly wiser, possibly inspired, intrigued and maybe not a little envious and in some happy cases you may be left with a compelling urge to go and do thou likewise.

Twelve years have passed since I wrote those lines and I read them again with the benefit of more than a decade of hindsight. I stand by what I wrote. The great truths of our wildlife and its management are eternal and the Hauxton project advances and matures like a fine wine. The dashing young thruster has become comfortably middle-aged, a Hauxton of pipe and slippers at ease with itself, the excitement of major new projects having given way to daily maintenance and fine-tuning. Will's Shoot has settled into an even tenor of its ways, its success proving that the thinking behind its creation was as inspired as we believed in the early days.

The changes we see are less in the wildlife and more in the people who have passed though the green iron gate for humankind is ephemeral, here today and who knows where tomorrow. Having reached their span of years some Hauxton disciples have strolled through far more imposing gates into the great reserve in the sky. Their friendly ghosts, dogs at heel or fishing rods on shoulder, haunt the shadows under the tall willows. Their names feature in the pages that follow and assure their immortality. It is no vain hope that Will's Shoot will outlive all of us who watched it grow and lent a hand: who could desire a more eloquent testament?

John Humphreys
Bottisham 2005

INTRODUCTION

I had been prompted for a year or two to enter my project at Hauxton Pits, for the Laurent Perrier Award. In 1988 I decided to apply, as it was twenty years since my original purchase of the area and it would be a good opportunity to put down on paper something of its development. For those twenty years I had been working to enhance the potential for game and wildlife on the site acquired at auction while I was still an art student. I had seen the enormous potential of these sixty-nine acres (28 hectares) of disused gravel pits, but had not realised that far more could be achieved than envisaged in my original dreams. During those years I held the dual role of keeper of the shoot and warden of the sanctuary. In my mind the relationship between the management of habitat for game or wildlife has always been inseparable. Both require a wide diversity of ecological conditions and so the development and management of the areas of woodland, water, marsh and arable were a great challenge. Hauxton is full of variety: from dry heath to wetlands, dense dark cover to light open spaces and soil conditions from fertile fields to dry sand or barren gault clay.

These conditions attract a wide variety of plants which support in turn many species of insects, a wealth of bird life and provide an ideal habitat for many species of lowland game and wildfowl. Whilst game species represent only the few which the keeper manages directly in order to produce a shootable harvest, his work creates the habitat and conditions required by so many other forms of wildlife which make up the rich tapestry of the British countryside. My ambition has been to produce a diversity of habitat not just to attract rare species but where the common ones are abundant; that on this tiny patch of England wildlife and game are not just a dream but a reality.

From bees to badgers, brimstones to bats, snakes to snipe, or frogs to pheasants, owls to orchids and kingfishers to carp, all thrive and there is something wonderful or new to be seen every day on a keepering round. Yes, of course such a haven will attract rarities and I was duly surprised and thrilled one day to come face to face with an osprey as it dived into a small pond, avoiding the overhead electricity wires, clasped a three pound carp between its outstretched talons and then made lazily away over the willows to sit on the skeleton of a dead elm and gorge itself. This bird whose scale is comfortable on a Scottish loch was so enormous when seen in the surroundings of Hauxton.

Being a practical countryman and artist, writing does not come naturally. However, it was a very good exercise to record for the Laurent Perrier presentation, in a concise and positive report, the main features of the work done over the years. This had to be a very factual and brief document written for the select panel of judges, each an expert in his field, any one of whom knew more than I ever will about their subject. However, I presented it in the spirit in which the place had evolved, as a DIY project with the help of innumerable friends.

To be awarded the first prize was thrilling and surprising, as previous award winners had been involved in either much larger scale projects or achieved acclaim for scientific studies which had national or international acclaim and application.

So here I am now, with the challenge to write a book on the subject. It could not be a 'how to do it' book but more the story of how I have enjoyed tackling this opportunity of a lifetime. I know my limitations as a writer and certainly the book will be far from high prose. I feel more comfortable with a letter writing style as if writing to you, the reader, as a friend enthusiastic about the countryside, wildlife and sport. This less formal approach makes for a story, punctuated by anecdotes about those involved, together with personal details and facts, costs or figures which, though relative to the year in question, are the sort of things I would find of interest in someone else's project.

The book is chronological, starting with the history and early days and later chapters telling of the development of the woodland for shooting and the lakes for fishing and wildfowl. Then specific game management techniques are discussed and a description of the spirit and atmosphere of a shooting day. Finally, a few random additional points complete the overall picture.

What is purposely absent is a chapter on conservation. This is because it is so fundamental to all that has been done and so is a thread that goes through all the other chapters. It is right that it cannot be isolated, as in the countryside it should be a positive consideration at all times. Every action will be to the benefit or detriment of some plant or species and so a wide perspective, not only for today but for years ahead, must be maintained. Man is privileged to have the opportunity to manage the environment but must, equally, accept responsibility for it.

So many people and friends have helped and though several are mentioned there has not been space to acknowledge all of them. There are so many important jobs which have been done at times by those with the necessary equipment or just the time and willingness to share themselves with my enthusiasm. Looking back over the thirty-five years a lot has been achieved but it could not have been done without the considerable and consistent help of family and friends.

The author, aged twelve, with tame jackdaw found as an abandoned fledgling.

1 · EARLY DAYS AND FORMATIVE YEARS

Boyhood Memories

Rushes, water, willow and sedge, such was the wilderness that supported a wealth of wildlife, wildfowl, warblers and waders. Through those reeds on a summer afternoon there stalked not only the elusive water rail but also a young boy called Will. A 'Dalesman' cane fishing rod was in his hand, his pride and joy. This was a present on his tenth birthday from his parents when all other small boys were collecting electric trains.

That was in the 1950s in the small Cambridgeshire village where I had been born in 1944. Little did I realise that later this same area of gravel pits would become such an important part of my life. At that age the only boundaries a boy knows are those at the limit of where his legs can carry him. What came naturally was the urge to move quietly and easily about the fields, woods and along the river and streams, one day clutching a jar for minnows or frog spawn, or another a box under my arm for birds' eggs or butterflies.

My parents allowed me great freedom as a boy, giving me responsibility for myself; possibly because I was the eldest of four children. As I was no saint I'm not sure this trust was justified, certainly St Christopher was on overtime watching over my safety on my travels. My father was wonderful in introducing me to aspects of country life, birdwatching or fishing, butterflies or shooting. He just opened the door and once through it the joys of all were there to notice, observe, appreciate and enjoy, whether captured in my mind or caught on rod and line. The country boy sees no distinction between the two, but the greater the individual's instinct to hunt, the greater is his inquisitive spirit to understand not only his quarry but its dependent environment and all of nature.

So my first visit to the gravel pits at the other end of the village one summer day was with my father, birdwatching, opening new horizons in every way. I was probably about ten years old at the time and had only known the area as the 'Pits', with its mysterious noises as machines droned through every season of the year. I passed the yard on my half mile walk home from the bus every day on my way back from school. Strangely, noises one grows up with, however intrusive to others, are accepted as part of the surroundings of home. The moaning and droning of the washing plant as it processed the freshly dug ballast fed by conveyer belt, running on squeaking bearings, up into a big cylindrical series of grids and sieves; then rattled and rotated until it was washed, to remove clay particles; then graded into clean fine sand, pea shingle, gravel or rejected flints, all separated into different heaps. There was a loader and lorries constantly chugging about. It was all quite noisy in a way but just part of life to me and ultimately it is not the noises or disturbance to our senses which cause aggravation but our attitude to them

It did not worry the colony of sand martins nesting nearby, the wagtails nesting in a disused pump or the wildfowl visitors in the winter – they saw the opportunities and what was good and did not worry about the noise or disturbance – maybe humans too can learn to have such attitudes to our environment.

We moved to a village four miles west when I was twelve where a larger house was to become home for us as more space was needed. I was away at school for my teens at Bradfield in Berkshire. For me a perfect school in a small village situated in a beautiful river valley. I always think of the time as being six fishing seasons rather than five years as I started there in the summer term, a term earlier than is normal to begin the school year. The River Pang, a chalk stream tributary of the Thames, flowed through the school grounds. Fly-fishing was a new form of sport for me. I learnt to rhythmically wave a small, light and very old greenheart rod, to cast a dry fly delicately on the water just ahead of the brown trout which thrived in the rich cool stream. Many boys fished and there was a successful club with a great hierarchy, depending on casting tests and seniority as to which stretches of river could be fished. In the summer term I fished every spare moment, everything about the chalk stream world fascinated me and my youth was not as 'misspent' as the masters thought at the time. 'Very expensive fishing fees for your son' was the summing up of one summer term by my housemaster who was accustomed to giving a full page report on a boy's achievement for the year!

Little did he, or I, know at the time that I was to paint rivers for my living in later years. He, Murray Argyle, was a most encouraging and supportive friend until his death a year or two ago.

It was about this time that my housemaster's attitude to my art changed but he normally considered 'art' to be a soft option. However, on the strength of a pub sign design I'd painted in class, mine being the 'Trout and Tankard', he agreed I had got more future in achieving art 'O' level than Latin. I believe the only thing 'soft' that had been touched was his spot for a beer, in retrospect very helpful for serious educational decisions!

Therefore another important and formative character in my life at Bradfield became the art master, Val Liddall, a man of great personality and strong character who, just coincidentally, fished and shot. In fact he was the master in charge of the school fishing and when I was reported to him for poaching on the colonel's water upstream, he angrily chastised me and said my real crime was that of being caught! The conclusion was that he put me in charge of the school fishing for my last two years. During that time I didn't get caught again and all the trout caught above or below our water were carried back in a bucket and stocked in our stretch. This is not a form of river management I now condone but for those two seasons the college water never fished better!

On Saturdays in the shooting season I used to cycle over to beat on shoots, to which he and the headmaster had been invited. One Saturday on a grand local estate the guns shot well below form after lunch. I noticed the elderly host was very displeased at tea afterwards. On the following Monday morning as I entered the art school the art master drew me aside and said his host had died on Saturday night. As a schoolboy with a fertile imagination I didn't please him by suggesting the two incidents were possibly related!

Val Liddall was an artistic inspiration to me, giving me enormous help and encouragement with his emphasis on drawing and painting technique. I learned so much, painting the local landscape and river in both watercolour and oils under his guidance. Not a man of the modern school but one who did have the power of positive teaching and a respect for the tradition of painting. He gave me confidence and enthusiasm to learn for the future from the Old Masters of the past.

So it can be seen that my love of nature and the countryside continued to develop: the enjoyment of absorbing all about me on the river bank and of how each individual plant, insect, fish or fowl relate; how seasons and weather changed the pattern of life in the water and on the banks; understanding that nothing in nature stands still, any habitat is constantly evolving, opening up opportunities for new species whilst causing others to decline.

The profound link between my artistic, sporting and wildlife interests were clearly evident in my teens. A passionate enjoyment and appreciation of all I experienced in the countryside was there at the beginning and I hope will be with me always. One regret I have educationally is that I never did biology, why not I can't imagine as a little scientific knowledge would have been invaluable.

Between nineteen and twenty-five I was at art school. A foundation year at Cambridge Art School, a three year scholarship to the Byam Shaw in London, followed by a further three years post graduate course at the Royal Academy School of Art in Piccadilly. It was at this time that my love of landscape painting developed and I also benefited from serious academic drawing classes – long days working in the dark life drawing room in what was the old stable and coach house area at the rear of Burlington House, where generations of great painters including Constable and Turner had also studied the complexities of drawing the human figure; the anatomical structure, the beauty of tone as light expresses form. These studies were helped also by visits on my own one day each week to draw in the Natural History Museum and by a course in 'comparative anatomy'. This course, by a professor from the Middlesex Hospital, drew attention to the exciting evolution of mammals and birds and their differences, but with so many similarities adapted for the environment in which they could thrive.

This was all tempered by the nearest thing to the country I craved while in London, cycling to and from art school through Hyde Park and along the Serpentine, noting the migrant wildfowl and strange visitors to the water there. To me the excitement of seeing a woodcock flighting over the traffic in Bayswater Road one November evening was far greater than some film star or celebrity I may have seen in Bond Street during the day!

The Auction

By the time I reached my last year at art school I had been married for four years to Gina who had been a fellow student at the Byam Shaw – a wonderful girl and it had been love at first sight. Her calm, quiet nature was a good influence on me and we shared interests in painting. We had a year old daughter, Jacquelyn, and were wondering where we'd move to live outside London after I completed the Royal Academy School course.

In January 1970, we visited my parents for the weekend and they mentioned that the old gravel pits were to be sold. Wisbeys, the local building firm, had completed extraction on the site and were offering various parcels of land for sale on which building was never a possibility as it was 'Green Belt' between two villages. Having had such an interest in this area as a boy I thought I'd enjoy revisiting the site, as I had not seen it since I was twelve. I took Judy, our household yellow labrador for a walk there on the Sunday afternoon.

An overcast cold, damp January afternoon is never likely to show such a place at its best. I was surprised at the extensive colonisation of willows which had grown on the ridges since I was a boy. These ranged from some thirty feet (9 m) on the eastern end to eight or ten feet (3 m) on the western side. This was a time section illustrating the period of digging from east to west.

There were no footpaths, just ridges with willows, furrows with water, some open glades where dry barren sand prevented growth other than grasses. A snipe zipped away up through the trees from a damp hollow of decaying leaves, six mallard quacked noisily as they rose resenting this rare intrusion to their daytime sanctuary. A family of long-tailed tits 'sip, sipped' along the tops of a row of willows, picking whatever little delicacies of food that were available on the buds and twigs at that lean time of year. Then Judy flushed a hen pheasant which departed with acceleration that is only possible of the true wily and wild.

The ridge and furrow pattern of extraction meant that in spite of a great area of water surface, there was actually little possibility of fish. Only in one or two areas where the gravel seams had been deeper did these ridges become submerged to

Aerial view of the old gravel pits at the time of purchase, 1970.

make shallow lagoons populated by a myriad of stunted rudd and perch. However, something instinctively kindled my interest as although I could not actually identify anything ideal for fishing or shooting, it was all so full of hidden potential. Certainly it was a rich area from the ornithological point of view. The great strength was that this area was very unusual as there had been no stipulation for reinstatement, backfilling or landscaping in the original planning permission to extract gravel. The area was just dug and then abandoned.

I had never even been to an auction of tables and chairs, let alone property. My curiosity therefore led me to arrange that I would return to Cambridge in the middle of the following week to go to the auction with my father. This was Wednesday 28 January 1970. The Farmers Club in Cambridge was packed and we sat at the rear of the large room. The first three lots were either unsold or sold for modest sums in spite of the extensive advertising and local press coverage. Rumour of corporations, the council or of government buyers, had not so far been evident. However, it was Lot 4 which would attract the most interest, as it did for me, wondering who would become the new owners of this area so rich in nostalgic memories of my boyhood.

The auctioneer was Douglas January, whose mother had lived next door to us in the village and whom I'd known for some years as his family were about my age and we had grown up together. I used to go fishing for minnows with his son, Richard, who was at school with me in Cambridge. His twin daughters were born the same day as me on 9 October 1944, a busy day for the local midwife as she peddled backwards and forwards from Hauxton to Shelford several times that day on her heavy black bike.

'An exclusive area of land comprising lakes and willow plantations formed as the result of gravel extraction, in all some sixty-nine acres' (28 hectares), such was the description of Lot 4. The bidding was spontaneous with bids from left, right and centre of the room. The atmosphere of the room, with a hundred or so people present, was charged as this, the main lot drew bids increasing by £500 from the starting price of £3,000. However having reached around £7,500 the pace eased and then came to a temporary halt and silence fell on the room.

I was surprised, as whilst having no knowledge of land values, let alone finances to consider buying, it was ridiculous that it could be sold for such a derisory sum – I could see such possibilities and potential in the site and in an instinctive fit I offered a further £250. Heads turned. Douglas January, a considerable character who enjoyed the pomp and ceremony of such an occasion, commanded the hall with 'Gentlemen, I ask you, are we to accept such a bid from the young man at the back?' A moment's silence and he did so with a stare of recognition.

By now Father was egging me on as the bid went against me at £8,000 from my £7,750. At this point I was puzzled as the auctioneer stated that the property 'was now on the market' – what were we all here for otherwise I thought! It was not until later that I learnt about reserves placed on Lots to ensure a minimum selling price. Anyway on I went with a shaky wave of my pencil which yesterday had been drawing a nude model at art school and today was committing £8,250 of money I didn't have. A silence as long as for ever and no further bids in spite of two askings and the hammer went down on the table. It resounded round the room but right through me.

I was asked for a cheque for ten per cent there and then, another rude shock of the auction room. I went out to the phone box in the street and telephoned my bank manager in Leicester. 'Is that the Mr Garfit, the art student in London?' he asked, after hearing my request for an immediate loan of £825, a fortune in itself at that time when a brand new Land Rover cost less. 'And what plans have you got for finding the other ninety per cent Mr Garfit?' was his next question. The Black Horse in the Lloyds stable was definitely neighing and pawing the ground at having his quiet afternoon so disturbed! However, he calmed down and agreed but wished to be kept informed within a few days of my plans. I wrote my cheque and answered questions put by the local press reporter, 'Art student buys sixty-nine acres of disused Gravel Pits' was soon to appear with a mixed impression of irresponsibility, eccentricity or madness – I have to accept there was an element of truth in this!

I then met Dr Frank Perring who was the underbidder on behalf of the Cambridge and Ely Naturalist Trust. His limit had been £8,000 but his enthusiasm matched his congratulations when he heard I was interested in maintaining and developing the area for wildlife and sport. His delight was that, whilst losing it as a reserve for the Trust, the funds could be used to secure some other area in the county threatened by adverse development. He later visited the area and gave me some good advice based on his considerable experience of reserve management.

So I limped back to London that evening in my little car wondering just how I was going to explain to Gina that I was the owner of these sixty-nine acres of abandoned pits. For an art student with a young wife and child life was not easy, as finances were not abundant to say the least. I clearly remember that hour and a half drive, with its mixed emotions not knowing whether I was thrilled or horrified at my foolishness. Gina took it, as with most of my ideas, with a calm and supportive spirit, with a greater faith in me than I perhaps had in myself.

History of the Site

Southern Cambridgeshire is a geological mixture, the chalk uplands to the south being the southern end of the East Anglian Heights, a chalk ridge with its name being only a comparative description when confined to the flats and fens of this part of England. The heavy calcareous clay soils, which cap the chalk ridge and cover much of western Cambridgeshire's hedgeless prairies, produce record crops of wheat.

In central Cambridgeshire the river valleys of the Cam and Rhee lie in gravel beds laid down as the great ice caps melted and receded north. The land at Hauxton lay on these gravel beds which are below a light loam soil. Beside the rivers the flood plains are of rich alluvial silt, traditionally lush watermeadows some of which still survive, protected from the plough by occasional flooding.

The land I had bought separated two villages. To the north is the pre-Doomsday village of Hauxton, at that time 'Hawkston', an area where Normans enjoyed the sport of falconry in the river fens perhaps. To the south is Harston, an old coaching stop on the A10, now with more traffic than ever but with only a few of the original Inns. A traditional village, however, its charm was not complimented by Rupert Brooke in his poem 'Granchester' when he wrote about local Cambridgeshire villages:

Ditton girls are mean and dirty
While in Harston there's none under thirty.

No wonder he was back in Granchester by ten to three,wondering if there was 'honey still for tea'!

Until the 1940s my land had been part of a mixed farm with a dairy herd. Fodder and root crops produced winter feed whilst the herd grazed in summer on the watermeadows behind the Norman church. Some cereals and grass leys produced a mixed pattern over the six or seven fields. There were old hedgerows with a few trees – an area typical of so much of English landscape at the time.

It was in the thirties and forties that Wisbey Brothers expanded their building business and started to extract gravel in the area on land the other side of the Lane in the village (this was later filled as a council tip and finally built on). They then moved on to the site which I now owned.

Gravel was dug over nearly thirty years, extraordinary by today's extraction programmes. However, the small Ransom 410 dragline digger was driven and maintained in pristine condition, the driver taking great pride in the engine at the rear of the cab, which shone without a trace of oil and his sandwiches would keep warm on it all morning until 'docky' time.

The method of digging was to work in rows with the progress of the dragline removing the top and subsoil which was hoisted out and dropped where the last row of gravel had been removed. Then the clean ballast was dug and loaded into a lorry, to be carted back to the washing plant where it was processed and graded. The ballast was dug either until below water level or until the underlying gault clay was reached. It was a shallow seam of gravel ranging from approximately eight feet (2.4 m) to as little as two feet (60 cm) deep. This method of working across the land left the ridge and furrow pattern which formed the basic landscape of the pits at the time of sale.

The extraction over such a long period, being dug only on demand, was either used by Wisbey's building company or sold to other local builders or customers. It was all very much a 'bucket and spade' operation and would be a quite unviable commercial proposition today.

Ambitions and Objectives

In the beginning there was no clearly defined objective. As I was still living in London in my final year of art school, I was not able to visit the site except at weekends and holidays. I had to learn about the area, walking and exploring every inch at every season, observing and understanding the unique qualities of this exciting place. The water table, which rose three or four feet (about a metre) in the winter months filling all the abandoned furrows, made ideal wildfowl habitat. The ridges, colonised with willow herb, rush and willows, were a natural habitat for warblers in the summer. I wanted to find the balance between maintaining the best of what existed whilst steering and tilting any devlopments to go hand in hand with nature and extend the diversity of habitat. I hoped that over a number of years I could maximise the potential – many features of which were originally hidden but became revealed as climatic or financial opportunities arose. The jungle of swamp, reed, rush and willow was rapidly overgrowing to occlude the light and exclude the wildfowl, it would soon become what in Norfolk is known as 'Carr'.

There were no tracks, not even a footpath on the whole area, I had no machinery and no finances available. However, what I did have was youth and enthusiasm and more than my share of energy. What I did not know then, but certainly do now, is that I had and was to have many more, very good friends whose energy, enthusiasm, time and care have enabled us to achieve together what I could never have done alone.

A typical part of the sixty-nine acres of abandoned, ridge and furrow, gravel workings purchased at auction.

The author, then an art student aged twenty-five, in 1970.

My interests were as a general naturalist, enthusiastic shot and angler. The link which evolved between sport participation and management was soon obvious. What also became obvious as my observations, understanding and experience developed, was the link between sport management and all wildlife management. This became and is now universally understood as 'conservation', a word rare in the countryside vocabulary at that time.

This symbiotic process of management soon revealed that the more one improves the habitat and conditions for game, then the more diverse the botanical range and variety of insects, butterflies and birds. All was equally true the other way round; as a glade of woodland was opened to allow light in for the orchids, another wild pheasant territory was created and game would benefit. Therefore it was not with two hats but one that I worked as Warden of the Sanctuary and Keeper of the Shoot; so too are all gamekeepers in the country. Whilst producing a shootable surplus of game as a crop, they are also the greatest network of sanctuary wardens, managing and conserving an enormous acreage of the British Isles. They are the unsung heroes of the conservation movement, supported not by public finances or subscription, but by private farmers and landowners.

It soon became clear that the area I had purchased had a very untidy boundary and there was only access on one side. I could see that for the future, whatever I was able to develop or achieve it would be wise to try, over a period of years when possible or prudent, to extend and improve the boundaries. There was an obvious line to the rear of the houses on the south and the A10 on the west. In the north the road would make a good natural boundary but three narrow areas of land belonged to three different owners. The village of Hauxton was my north-eastern boundary with many indentations as groups of houses were built and plots of varying depths had been developed. A small rough four acre (1.6 hectare) field, on which a pony or two grazed, bit into the south-eastern corner. Now, after long, patient but friendly negotiations, some nine separate contracts and conveyances between 1970 and 1993, the long twenty year game of Monopoly has been completed. Fourteen conveyances of small pieces of land to extend surrounding gardens have simplified other boundaries and provided much of the finance required to purchase the larger area of farmland. The extra land purchased was eighteen acres (7.8 hectares) and total sold less than one, therefore making the total area in the region of eighty-seven acres (35 hectares) today.

Financial Restrictions

Following my purchase of the pits, finances were to say the least difficult. A considerable overdraft meant I had no working capital and only slowly, as funds could be saved or the kind bank manager from Lloyds be pressed for a further loan, could contractors be employed for major development stages of work through the years or machinery purchased.

Later, finances became a little easier and a cash flow evolved as one by one each enterprise produced income to be ploughed back or repay loans. No sooner had my friendly bank manager relaxed with a little confidence and credibility for the success

The Stages of Development of the Hauxton Pits

1cm=50m

1	1970	Purchase, at auction, of sixty-nine acres (28 hectares) of disused gravel pits.
2	1971	Purchase 'London Road Field', four acres (1.6 hectares)
3	1971	Make the H-shaped clearing in the main block of woodland
4	1972	Purchase 'The Lane Field', four acres (1.6 hectares)
5	1976	Construct Carp Lake, Lodge Lake and four other ponds
6	1979	Construct the Horseshoe Lake
7	1985	Purchase tenancy of Main Road Field (the freehold was included in original auction 1970)
8	1987	Purchase middle part of Church Road Field, 1.8 acres (0.7 hectares)
9	1987	Construct scrape area
10	1988	Purchase tenancy of corner part of Church Road Field, 1.6 acres (0.65 hectares)
	1988	Purchase freehold of corner part of Church Road Field
11	1989	Purchase land adjacent to yard, 1.5 acres (0.6 hectares)
12	1993	Purchase Mascall's Field

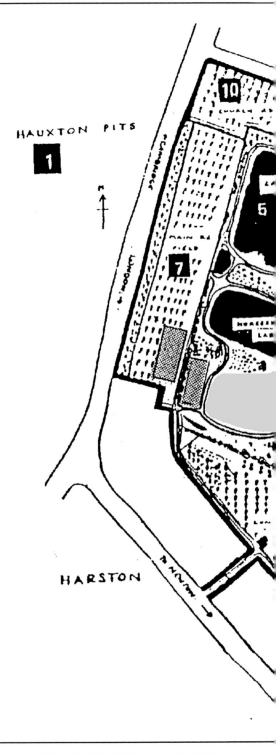

HAUXTON PITS

HARSTON

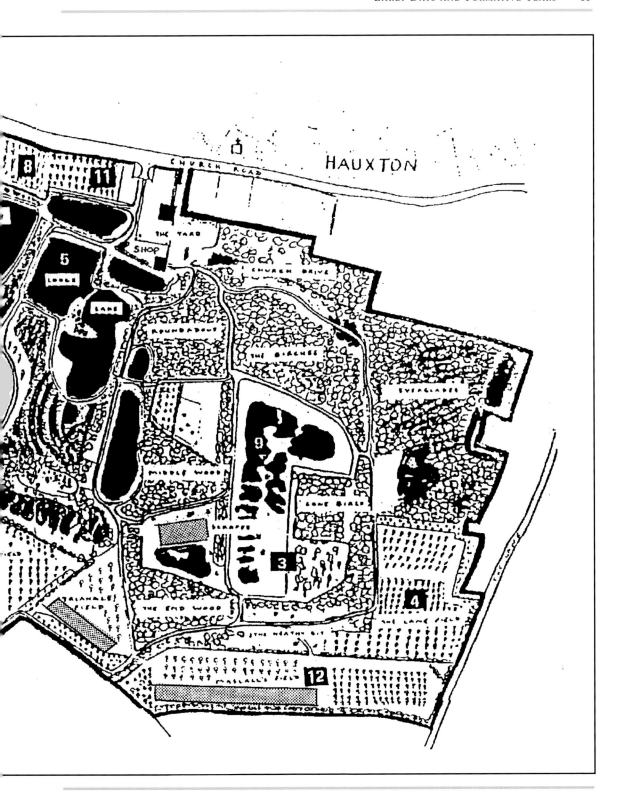

of the last scheme, than I had a larger more expensive one in my mind for the future. I did find that my policy of budgeting for a larger loan than I envisaged and of over estimating the time it would take to repay meant that, whilst overworking the manager's heart beat, it did make it easier to maintain credibility, while getting the job done properly.

The managers at Lloyds continually trade up to more senior posts and each retiring one must have left me a better 'end of term' report because each new one has been the more supportive. The manager at the time makes an annual visit in the summer from Leicester. After lunch we visit the pits where an afternoon feeding carp, trout or young duck of the year, watching swifts and swallows hunting insects over the lakes or a kingfisher diving for carp fry whilst anglers enjoy their sport, make a more pleasant client's visit than to a factory or office.

There is always some new development whether financial, ecological, business or sporting, and it is never easy for him to make a formal report the next day at the bank. Most of the values are those that enrich the human spirit rather than those that can be defined on a ledger in the Bank, as either capital or income.

However, he has never refused me a further loan!

First Steps

It is difficult to recall what were the first positive actions I took to improve things. I certainly remember that on the strength of seeing the odd wild pheasant I soon made two straw feeders which I designed to keep pheasants occupied and fed for the week while I was in London. These comprised of a number of four foot (1.2 m) long sticks hammered into the ground about six to nine inches (approx 20 cm) apart in a circle of six foot (1.8 m) diameter. This was then filled with straw and layers of wheat tailings given to me by a farmer friend. The pheasants could scratch the straw out from the bottom and as the heap of straw dropped so the corn could be found – a form of natural straw hopper.

Each weekend I'd refill with the straw (by then spread around the outside of the circle of sticks) and more corn. By the activity and evidence I could see there were perhaps a few more pheasants than I'd at first thought. This encouraged me to go further and start a little vermin control. One day there might even be a little shoot.

A man had achieved a shoot on a small acreage in Hampshire and my love and enthusiasm for pigeon shooting had led me to meet this great man himself. His name was Archie Coats. He was a legend in his own lifetime, known to all those with a sporting passion for pigeons. He was the father of modern pigeon shooting and through his book *Pigeon Shooting*, his lectures and his appearances on the Eley stand for many years at Game Fairs, he was known to many who pursue the wood pigeon

My old friend, the late Archie Coats, with Prue, his wife and constant support.

from every wood, hedgerow and field in the British Isles. A man of immense charisma, character and charm, with a dedication to shooting that in the field, combined his concentration of mind, agility of footwork and spontaneity of gunmounting, made him the most accurate and effective game shot I've ever been privileged to see. I watched him on so many occasions whether shooting pigeon, pheasants, grouse, partridges in Spain or wildfowl in Rumania. A shot who was always so alert that not only did he seldom miss but never missed a safe opportunity. I remember him fondly as my 'sporting father'.

Archie and Prue, his dedicated wife and 'patron saint' of all shooters' wives, ran the most remarkable shoot of thirteen acres around their house, Towerhill. As I frequently visited them I would usually find myself doing some little job before going out pigeon shooting. Whether volunteered or co-opted, the Major's instructions would be clear to the nearest handful of corn by a bush, or whether straw on a certain feed should be kicked to the left or the right. I would be quizzed on how many and of the precise location of pheasant droppings I'd seen, or whether a rat had taken any bait from beneath a corrugated iron sheet three paces from the drinker by the second feed in the 'Remise'. The reader may understand something of the Major's attention to detail on such a personalised shoot around the house. Needless to say, every square yard was of ideal habitat which was the key to a pheasant's five star accommodation whether resident or visitor. If the latter then they usually became the former. A patchwork of Christmas trees of varying ages for roosting and shelter, open rough areas such as the dock field, scrubby patches of bushes, coppice and ivy clad thorns such as the Remise and small cultivated areas of wild strawberries – a valuable crop of *fraise du bois* which in winter were attractive sunny glades with straw between the rows in which the pheasants could scratch and while away the day until feed time again. It was not until later that I was privileged to be invited to shoot there; this was not to be awarded until helping as described for at least ten years! However, what I had seen was that it was possible to have a shoot on a small area providing, and this is the key to it all, that the habitat for game is right, not just good but very good, producing roosting, shelter, food, water, nesting sites and all in a vermin free home. So this was a most encouraging challenge for me with Hauxton's seventy acres (28 hectares), a veritable Holkham, Elvedon or Sandringham in proportion compared with Towerhill's thirteen (5.2 hectares).

It was not long before I heard of a man who used to act as an informal bailiff while the gravel pits were active. Roger Jeeves lived in a bungalow in the village and had moved there with his wife, Millie, son Simon and Honey, his yellow labrador to be near the pit. He was in his late thirties and in those days was a dedicated wildfowler; although employed at a local paper works he would migrate north at weekends to the Norfolk coast as regularly as the wildfowl which frequented it. It was soon apparent that here was a good friend of the pits and soon to become a good friend to me. He was enthusiastic to help in any way and particularly knowledgeable about the duck and their flight lines in every wind condition and state of the moon. He knew the runnels of water and ridges of reeds better than the veins and hairs on the back of his hand. A traditionalist and a man who with so many happy memories behind him in the pits was, however, reluctant to welcome change. My visions and development have worried him on several occasions. On many a night it was not the moon and the duck flighting to or from the pit that had kept him awake but his fear that there would be less, whilst my ambition was that there should be more. Together we have achieved the many improvements happily.

Other early memories are of a visit by an old friend, Mike Ingram, a chap with a kindred boyish enthusiasm and pioneering spirit. He'd had thirty jobs in his first year after leaving school and then as a photographer set off on an optimistic expedition to cross South America on foot. However, the first stop on the boat crossing the Atlantic was at the Canary Islands where he disembarked to see the sights and, yes, you've guessed it, he missed the boat. It then cost him his expedition

Roger, always keen on his dog work, here seen with Jess and Anna.

budget to fly to South America to meet and recover his luggage and photographic equipment, which had still been on board the steamer! Later, having settled down a bit he achieved a PhD in marine biology at Liverpool; now married with a large and lovely family on the Isle of Man, where he became a leading international consultant in the aquaculture and fish farming business before moving on to other entrepreneurial enterprises.

However, in our early twenties we set out to pioneer the jungles of Hauxton. We hacked a path into the large area of solid willow woodland on the eastern side, winding from glade to glade. We found an area with young silver birch which were becoming choked by the willows and sallow; we cleared the willow by digging them up manually, as if just cut off they would have regrown with even greater vigour than before. Over thirty years later that same area has no willows and is an attractive group of mature birches – no immense ecological achievement perhaps after so much hard work but an addition to the diversity and beauty of the woodland.

I met a young man who was a knowledgeable ornithologist and was interested in ringing birds for the British Trust for Ornithology. The BTO have a strict code of conduct on this and ringing can only be done by trained and approved ornithologists. For a number of years Julian Limentani set his mist nets and produced some remarkable information on the ages and movements of both migrant and resident species. Of the migrants, sedge, reed, willow and garden warblers, chiffchaff and blackcaps were the most numerous.

Recoveries were fascinating, a reed warbler from near Lisbon in Portugal, a sedge warbler controlled in a net in the same path four years running – just how far had that little bird flown on migration possibly to Africa and back four times. Yellowhammers and blackbirds living for four, five, even six years. A long-tailed tit controlled at Wicken Fen in 1972, only about twenty miles from Hauxton, but a long way for a tit one thinks of as a resident.

Perhaps the most interesting sight was the day Julian caught a goldcrest and a firecrest in the net at the same time enabling an 'in the hand' comparison of the two smallest birds in the British Isles. The firecrest certainly does have a brilliant crest of orange, whilst the goldcrest is of yellow gold. However, when the crest of the goldcrest is stroked the wrong way, from back to front, the colour inside is as orange as the firecrest. Therefore it is only the outer end of the tiny feathers on its head that are gold. A little marvel of nature one would never have ever known until the birds were caught for ringing purposes.

There were species which were rare then and have not been recorded recently such as the grasshopper warbler, red-backed shrike and Jack snipe. Otherwise of the ninety-seven species recorded on the BTO register of 1972/3, including sixty-nine breeding species, most are still to be seen, some species increasing, others holding their own against a general decline. An ornithological census of birds breeding in Cambridgeshire in 1989 produced a list of just over four hundred pairs of birds breeding on the site. This, from one visit in July, included forty-nine species.

In the early 1970s, Julian erected many nesting boxes for tits and small birds as natural holes for nesting sites were not available in the comparatively young willow woodland. These were successfully used for several seasons but one year a weasel saw the easy opportunity for food and visited the bird boxes, stealing most of the nestlings before it could be caught.

For two or three years after Wisbeys had sold the old pits they somehow never moved out of the yard or stopped trading from there. It seems a strange situation to look back on but in fact it was mutually convenient, as all on the site were of such help to me. There was no gravel being dug but it was brought in by lorry from active pits the other side of Cambridge and sold in small quantities to builders and farmers locally. The two lorry drivers, John and Harold, were both local men I'd known  for many years. In fact Harold had worked for my father when we lived at Hauxton, helping in the garden. He was a great countryman and something of a poacher with stories of rabbits he'd caught up pollarded willows on the fen when the river was in flood. I shall always remember at the early age of six or seven, digging a deep hole in the garden down to the water table. I had erected a warning notice 'DEEP HOL'. It was Harold who in his country accent said 'that there 'ole should 'ave an 'e'.' So where it gained an 'e' it lost an 'h' – no wonder I've never been able to spell.

As is so often the way in local communities everybody is connected in some way. John, the other lorry driver was the brother-in-law of Margaret who helps Mother and now both Mother and Gina in the house. He was always arriving back in the yard with surplus building materials from sites and instead of dumping them he would store them for later use for bridges, roads, fences or dusting shelters. Old kerbs, sheets of corrugated iron, bricks or timber – we were seldom short thanks to John.

There was a small wooden hut in the yard where a 'tortoise' cast iron stove was kept red hot, fuelled by broken pallets or rubbish; black smoke belched from the rusty iron chimney whenever Ken, 'the boy', stoked it. Old Jack Wisbey, reading his tabloid, sat comfortably in an armchair which he shared with mice living in the stuffing. Ken, the boy, was in his forties but had started working there when he left school at fifteen and as nobody younger had ever joined the employment of Wisbey Brothers, he was always called 'the boy' by his elderly employers. There were five Wisbey brothers, all involved in the business. The pace of life was steady and while Stan was the Chairman of the Company and assumed all the responsibilities about which he seemed to constantly worry and moan, the other four brothers had a very laid back approach without a worry in the world. However, they could seldom agree and so decisions were difficult and usually deferred until another day. I would never have bought the land at all if it had not been sold by auction, as a negotiated sale could never have been agreed by all five directors. An example of this was the difficulty I had in purchasing the old grey Ferguson 35 tractor. These Fergy 35s were perhaps the most successful tractor of all time and there was hardly a farm in the forties and fifties which did not have one. In fact these little character tractors are still in use on hill farms, smallholdings and crofts today, as useful as they ever were. However, when I was offered this tractor, a 1957 model, which had been used for loading gravel or levelling building sites for fifteen years, and was in a working but rough order, I agreed to buy it. It then took two full directors' meetings to decide if I was to pay £75 for the tractor, with or without the old rotovator. A month later in spite of all five brothers still not in full agreement, the sale was completed. I was then the proud owner of my first piece of agricultural machinery. It ran well but as children on a building site had conducted certain surgical operations on it, the dashboard was blind having had all the gauges gouged out and most of the electrical intestines removed. However, now my Fergy is thirty-five by name but forty-five by age, working many hours each year grass cutting, flailing undergrowth, towing trailers or augering out holes for tree planting. The most versatile and useful machine I've ever bought.

More implements were begged, borrowed or bought later from farmer friends or farm sales and also a larger tractor for heavy work, a 1963 Fordson Super Major. This is another great stalwart of British agriculture. I knew this tractor had had very little use and was in 'as new' condition, though ten years old when it was for sale by auction, on the retirement of the farmer on the hill. It cost me £600 in 1973, a price which was high for a tractor of that age at the time, but I knew it was a bargain. It too is still working regularly though more than forty years old.

It has been modest investment in machinery each year that has enabled a lot of work to be achieved and so, with ploughs, cultivators, rotovators, grass cutters and flails, trailers, augers and lifting equipment, I'm well set up for most jobs on the reserve, shoot, fisheries or tree plantation that have been developed over the years.

The only piece of equipment of which I did not really make full use was the old Ransom dragline digger I bought, in its retirement, with my neighbour. We paid £300 which was really its scrap value but it did work and I had lessons from the original driver who, patiently on a Sunday morning, would take me through the complications of heavy levers and foot pedals which controlled enormous drums and winches to cast out the bucket and then retrieve and lift it with a full load. The tracking gears, the slewing mechanism for controlling movement of the whole cab and jib to turn left or right, together with the delicacies of the Perkins diesel engine were shared with the operator in the cab. So many co-ordinations give me great respect for all machine operators I see in action, working with dexterity and skill.

It soon became obvious that if it ever broke down it would either be impossible or very costly to repair and we sold it with some relief before either eventuality.

2 · Woodland

The Original Willow Woodland – The Four Ages of Willows

At the time I acquired the land in 1970 the area could be thought of in two halves which coincidentally were divided by the line of electricity poles running north to south across the site. To the west were the later diggings of long narrow fingers of waste gravel ridges with water in the furrows. Some of this area was colonised by the youngest and first stage of willows, feathered saplings no more than about five to fifteen feet (1.5 to 4.5 m) tall. It was beyond the fresh dug bare gravel stage but not yet at a stage it could be thought of as woodland. It is in fact perhaps one of the most valuable from an ornithological point of view, as there is still enough open water for wildfowl and waders whilst sallow and willow scrub produce an ideal habitat for warblers, tits and all small insectivorous species.

By contrast the eastern block of land, some thirty-five acres (14 hectares), comprised of more advanced willow woodland. Part of this was at the second stage, at what foresters call 'thicket'. This really was willow woodland at its most dense (my beater friends would say it is all at that stage all the time!). This area had been levelled after the gravel had been dug and abandoned. It was then colonised by willows which are such profuse seeders. In June, like whisps of feathery cotton wool the willow down carries millions of minute seeds downwind of the parent trees. There are, I understand from arboricultural botanists, a great number of willow species. However Mother Nature can do nothing to inhibit promiscuity and consequential hybridisation so willows from seed will rarely be true to one species and always have traces of a number of clones. Only if grown from cuttings will the willow propagate true to the parent tree. This is easily done with any willow twig, stick or post stuck into moist ground, so enthusiastic is the willow to take root. I have sometimes seen people make cheap fence posts of this wood only to find the following spring the whole fence comes to life. This trick can of course be used intentionally and will make a virtually instant hedge or barrier of willow posts, especially when interwoven diagonally with long withy wands with their butt end in the ground. We have made duck hides like this which can be maintained permanently with a little trimming each year. They are most effective and look very natural throughout the year beside the pond. I use the straight willow coppice growth as sticks, slit in the top to hold the gun numbers, as shooting pegs. If not removed at the end of the season they too have been known to grow. Guns the following season can be imagined groping into a willow bush to see what number it is.

This prolific seeder therefore produces a dense growth of young seedlings which is what had happened on the bare levelled area of some ten acres. It would have been like this in the 1960s when, post myxomatosis, there were few if no rabbits in the area, neither were there any deer. Either or both if present would have grazed the young willow seedlings but in their absence there was nothing to inhibit their growth and development until they themselves, in their bid for survival, fought for light as they grew up, and competed for moisture and nutrient as their roots grew down. Nature is tough and it is only the strong and most vigorous which survive, such is the way of the woodland world. Ultimately any mature wood can only support comparatively few trees per acre by natural regeneration or for that matter by forestry planting. Therefore from the earliest days as seedlings, the young trees compete and the weaker ones are occluded and die as the tree canopy of the strongest closes over them. From originally hundreds of seedlings per square yard, by the thicket stage (at ten to twenty feet (3 to 6 m) the number of willows are reduced by over ninety per cent, perhaps to one every three square yards. By the time of maturity at about seventy or eighty feet (over 20 m) high there may be only one tree on perhaps forty to fifty square yards or about one hundred per acre (two hundred per hectare) at most.

What has been fascinating to me is that the fast growing willows have given me a crash course in woodland development and in the period of just over thirty years I have seen trees through all ages. A salutory lesson of the comparative ages of trees and man is seen when a willow uprooted in a gale is cut up. To count back thirty-five of the tree rings will illustrate how small the tree was in 1970 at the time I acquired the site, aged twenty-five.

The most mature part of the area was on the eastern end where, beyond those of the thicket stage, there were the oldest trees where digging was completed in perhaps the 1950s and this area became known as 'The Everglades', towering mature willows of seventy to eighty feet (over 20 m) growing on mounds and islands with damp or watery steamy hollows in between. In the summer it appears to have a micro climate of its own being hot and humid, full of mosquitoes the size of tarantulas. Well, maybe I do exaggerate a little but that is how the Council Officer for Health said he'd had them described by complaining people in adjacent houses one particularly jacuzzi summer.

The final growth stage which now completes the picture is of the old willows which stand covered in ivy. The pheasants like the warm, sheltered roosting and pigeons feed, in late winter, on the berries. Wrens, tits, spotted flycatchers and tree creepers are among birds which nest in the dark sanctuaries within the secret canopy of the ivy.

There is something of a management dilemma in that the ivy, whilst being a good additional habitat for many species of wildlife, will later cause the premature fall of the tree. Solid rooted species like oak and ash will happily carry ivy for many years without detriment but willows, growing shallow rooted in gravel on a high water table, will not be able to withstand gales. The wind resistance is increased by the ivy as a ship with full sail and eventually it will blow over.

On balance I consider by leaving ivy on the trees the natural cycle produces a wider and more varied ecological environment. The willow trees are of no financial value and so my only consideration is the benefit or loss to game and wildlife. As a tree falls the light is allowed to penetrate the ground producing a small glade and later another generation of growth will develop. Interestingly enough it is seldom willow which regenerates, but first bramble, then elder and thorn with the occasional ash or sycamore. The latter I usually cut out as it is an aggressive coloniser and of no value to game and little to wildlife compared with other species.

An old friend, Robert Reynolds, who worked in Cambridge running a family garage business would often escape his office in an afternoon to let off steam and help with work in the woods. He owned a chain saw and this enabled so much more progress whether clearing unwanted trees or cutting pathways through the woods. I hope Robert's saw was not too worn out by the time investment was made in a chain saw of my own. It is now a vital piece of equipment for woodland management.

1971 Clearing

Apart from the few pioneering paths through the dense woodland of the thirty-five acre (14 hectare) eastern area, the site was one solid, mostly impenetrable, block. If there had been hundreds of pheasants in such cover they could never have made any sport whether driven or even walked up. It occurred to me that if I was to open it up by creating rides and a clearing, it was possible to make a series of smaller coverts with space to drive pheasants from one to another, across the clearing and over the guns.

The design of the shapes of the instant woodland which would remain and the strategy as to how they could be driven in the future was critical. It is important for pheasants, when flushed, to have enough space and time in which to take off and to reach optimum height and speed to produce the best sport. Shooting pheasants in large blocks of woodland with rides alone for guns to stand is not sufficient. Most pheasants will naturally run ahead of the beaters and flush too close to the line of guns, producing poor or unshootable birds. There are two ways of solving this: one is to have a clearing and space as I planned within the wood; alternatively, and the most viable in commercial woodland because less trees need to be felled, is to have two rides, one for the standing line of guns and another parallel, ideally some seventy to eighty yards (about 70 m) in front of the guns. This flushing ride can be most effective, particularly with the use of sewelling, a line with strips of coloured polythene hanging from it, supported three foot (1 m) off the ground every few yards by a stick. This should extend the length of the flushing ride and be activated by a chap at one end jiggling it. The objective is for pheasants to run no further forward and so take to the wing at this point, flying forward above the tree tops reaching maximum height and speed as they cross the line of guns. Even on flat ground this can produce good sport particularly if the trees of the wood are tall. The most successful use of this technique that I've experienced, making good birds in a big wood is at Bartlow in East Cambridgeshire. The big wood there is used as a reservoir for birds in the early part of the season producing good outside drives, when birds are fed or blanked out and flown back home. However, later in the season the wood is shot by blanking three-quarters of it round into the fourth corner section. The pheasants are then driven over the guns from a wide flushing ride where an extensive, newspaper-on-sticks sewelling line inspires the birds to fly high over the ninety foot (27 m) ash trees where guns are placed in small glades, shooting through windows of the branch canopy. This can produce some very exciting and testing sport.

Back on the mini scale of Hauxton, I finally decided on an H shaped clearing with access or feed rides through the adjoining outside woodland. In all the H shape was of approximately four acres (1.6 hectares) and it was a considerable job to clear and burn an area of this size with two small drotts. One of these mini bulldozer-like machines worked ahead with a normal four in one bucket, pushing down the twenty to thirty foot tall willows and the second drott with a fork bucket would lift or push them in heaps to the fires. The actual shape and orientation of clearing was pioneered by me with a flag walking ahead of the first drott through the jungle, having established the angle of the sun ahead to guide me for the first swathe.

The whole operation was slow and in retrospect I would have probably achieved the job more economically with larger bulldozers which would have been more costly per hour but would have taken much less time. However, in those days at only £3 an hour for drott and driver, the work was slow but sure. There were frequent breakdowns as both these B 100 machines were old and maintenance had not been a high priority. Both drivers, Noel and Peter, were masters at on site repairs. The tool kit was minimal, comprising a heavy hammer and long iron bar, one end flattened to double as screw driver or lever. Brute force rather than mechanical skill was the technique these robust workhorses responded to best. These boys would not I fear have been employed in a sewing machine factory!

They persevered and after about three weeks all the trees were grubbed up and burnt on enormous fires of intense heat. As each load was shunted on to the fire a cloud of black soot and ash exploded into the air enveloping the man and machine. There were no cabs or protection and both drivers were filthy as the soot and sweat was smeared across their arms and faces. The scene was a miniature version of the films seen of the clearance of South American rain forests, but the destruction and loss of forest on a world scale in the Southern Hemisphere is very different from my mini constructive ecological clearance in the Northern (this is the nearest I venture into international environmental politics!). Later the roots were grubbed out by the heavy steel tines on the back of the drotts. On the scale of Hauxton, this was a dramatic transformation producing a clearing which appeared even larger than it was. In reality, each leg of the irregular 'H' was about 150 yards (140 m) long and the cross piece about the same, a design which produced the maximum edge of woodland. This edge was very stark at this stage as the section through the original

1971: The drotts making the H-shaped clearing in the willow woodland.

wood left tall, straight and thin willows standing as a palisade fence surrounding the clearing. However, after a year or two the edges soon softened as the undergrowth grew at ground level and willow branches leaned out into the new space. So many birds as well as pheasants thrive on the woodland margin and this newly created 'edge effect' was soon to make a positive contribution to the whole ecology of the woodland area.

Two enormous fires still smouldered at either end of the clearing and there were piles of ash higher than the machines, ideal for good bird dusting baths. I asked Peter, one of the drivers, to tip heaps of this along the woodland edges, a chain apart, to make 'all mod cons' bird dusting facilities.

One doesn't seem to talk or think in chains today but it was a good countryman's measure of distance. Twenty-two yards, the original convenient length for a cricket pitch, is perhaps one of the few uses of a chain today. It was a good pre-metric measure: ten chains made a furlong (220 yards / 200 m), as we used to run races at school. A furlong was originally a 'furrow long' when ploughed, a chain wide was an acre, the area a man and a pair of horses would plough in a day. Furlongs still live on in the horse racing world of course, but few children today would know that there are eight furlongs to a mile. 'What's a mile?' children will possibly ask in the next generation.

This major development cost in the region of a thousand pounds, a lot of money at the time, but it was the key to producing the instant possibility of a shoot and was the most important factor in achieving it. The separate woods now make five or six drives and a full morning's shooting early in the season as individual drives; later it is more successful to blank one into another making fewer but longer drives to catch out the more wily cocks which otherwise run out.

Glades

The open clearing itself is not just a space across which to drive the pheasants but is important as a contribution of light to the habitat required by game.

The ecology of any wood is enhanced enormously by having open spaces where the sunlight can penetrate the woodland floor. At Hauxton this effect has been produced in a number of ways. The rides and large clearing have been the greatest single contributor, creating what I see as an 'open and shut' habitat. This is where cover, shelter and roosting of the woodland surrounds cosy, warm open spaces where game can feed, dry in the sun after a shower and nest in the suitable vegetation. In the spring cock pheasants will display and take up territories in the glades. Ground cover will make good nesting sites for the hens and the warmth of the glades produces abundant insect life for young pheasants and all birds feeding nestlings in the spring. A solid dense dark woodland will not provide this vital variety so important to wildlife. On a two-day Game Conservancy small shoot management course a few years ago in May, I completed my woodland talk by two minutes silence. As the party of eighty, keepers, farmers and shoot managers, stood in the clearing, the noise of birds singing all round seemed deafening – from the willow warblers and chiffchaffs in the top branches to the territorial crowing of the cock pheasants on the ground, from the wrens, robins and dunnocks in the thick of the bushes and brambles to the mallard calling their ducklings on an adjacent pond. Everywhere were the sounds of healthy, open woodland of diverse habitat surrounding the glades where the edges were light and sheltered and warm in the sunshine. 'This,' I explained, 'is the sound of woodland which will hold pheasants.'

Pheasants will stay pottering about all day from wood to glade seeking sun or shelter without the urge to get out of the wood and wander miles across surrounding fields possibly ending up in your neighbour's coverts by the evening.

Apart from rides and clearings there are ponds in the wet areas which are ideal for wildfowl through the year and again the edges are loved by pheasants, a bird of the marsh as much as the wood. Then there are areas of willow coppiced by thatchers. There are two thatchers at Hauxton, each has his own area of woodland to manage. With my guidance, areas within the woods are cut to ground level and as this commenced when the original willows were young, it was easy to achieve. Each year the vigorous shoots from each 'stool', as a stump is known, will grow four or five feet (about 1.5 m). After four years they are long and lean, the thickness of a spade handle. They are cut with a bill hook at the base of the stool and then tied in bundles. Later they are split in half and half again and yet half again so making long thin,

pliable wands used when bent and twisted to secure the straw and are known as 'spars' or 'pegs'. The fine ones or 'sways' are used for the ridge and when latticed and pegged the beauty of the thatcher's craft protects a cottage from the weather and enhances its charm for many years to come. (In this area willow is used but in other parts of the country hazel is more abundant and frequently coppiced for use by the thatcher.)

The result of this coppicing is an open glade for one year, with progressive density of low bush to taller thicket, until cut again. This is light and airy and ideal woodcock habitat and there is a patchwork of coppice now over many areas of the woodland. It is a particularly suitable use of ground below electricity wires which must not have trees growing up amongst them or they will short the electricity to the ground. On occasions this has happened and the supply to the whole village is cut off. Such a drama then follows, with teams of electrical engineers driving about the woods, day or night, winter or summer, causing considerable disturbance. I now arrange that each year in February, after the shooting season, but before the arrival of migrant warblers, the Electricity Board contractors who cut away branches likely to offend in the coming year, complete their work and this usually prevents disturbance during the rest of the year. It was the regrowth on the stumps left by the Electricity Board men that gave me the idea of turning the area below the wires into willow coppice. This has three advantages, the value to the thatchers, the reduction of work necessary by the Electricity Board contractors and the consequential reduced risk of untimely disturbance to the woods.

The corridors through woodland under electricity lines can therefore be seen as a positive contribution producing both an asset in real terms and another glade with long edges like a ride. Unlike a ride, however, I would not recommend standing guns under wires and personally feel psychologically inhibited, for fear of being sizzled like a fly in the ultraviolet light trap in the butcher's shop on contact with a live wire! In reality I believe electricity cables are made of stronger stuff than to be in any way threatened by tiny soft lead shot and I have never heard of an electricity cable being brought down by shooting.

Telephone wires are altogether more tender and are very easily damaged even if not broken. I recall accidentally shooting a telephone wire when killing a pheasant above it in a snow storm in Dumfriesshire a number of years ago. I was very

concerned that the few outlying cottages up the glen were cut off the phone when they were about to be snowed in. I was just wondering how to muster help after the drive had finished when out of the snow storm came the most unlikely vehicle slithering and sliding along the lane. Yes, a little yellow GPO van. I thought this sort of coincidence only happened in children's books like Noddy or TV programmes like Trumpton. I stopped it – not exactly at gun point – and was relieved not only to meet a cheerful and helpful engineer, but to find he'd got a ladder on the roof and equipment on board to mend the wire. When I pointed to the limp wire, trailing in the snow from the pole each end, I didn't have to mention the obvious cause. A contribution to his favourite charity, probably some bar in Lochmaben, eased both my conscience and the plight of those cut off. It was accepted with a knowing wink and a smile and having completed the repair, he strapped the ladder back on the van and drove off into the blizzard. Would one get the same co-operation from BT today?

So the large block of thirty-five acres (14 hectares) has become a patchwork of woodland with glades, ponds and areas of coppice linked by arterial rides. The rides are not straight and boring, but curved so the beauty is visually improved and certainly the scale is psychologically increased. Because one can never see far from any one point, it is difficult to judge the size of the area or keep a sense of direction. Friends shooting there who come from large farms or grand acres of estates can be totally disorientated by the end of the morning's shooting on an area no larger than their smallest field.

I came across two men walking along a ride one day and when I asked if I could help, they explained that they were sorry but they were lost. I told them that the land was private and disturbance was not to the benefit of the wildlife. This they appreciated and were very polite and asked to be directed to the gate. When asked who they were they said they were from the Ordnance Survey producing maps! I pointed out that they hadn't demonstrated any great aptitude for the job, being lost on my little patch. I led them to the gate and directed them to the main road, suggesting they carried a compass and watched the sun when they left home next day. On occasions a keeper needs a lot of patience and diplomacy to maintain a sense of humour.

Woodland Management and Improvements – Light is Life

Having established the basic layout of the woodland for shooting, the next task was to consider how to improve it further for the holding of game. Willows are far from ideal trees for pheasant covers but they do have some advantages (being an optimist I tend to look for positive advantages rather than despair about disadvantages and problems). The willow with its long narrow leaves has a light canopy, allowing more light to filter through than almost any other hardwood species. The essence of life in a wood is light. Reduce the light by a dense canopy and life below, botanically and entomologically, will be almost proportionally reduced until in extreme cases, as in dense pine and spruce plantations, there is no light and no life below, just a barren carpet of pine needles.

Another advantage of the willow is that it grows fast and when in a wood or even a group, will grow tall. Mature willows at Hauxton reach a height of seventy to eighty feet (aprox. 25 m). This I know accurately because when pigeon flighting I have twelve six-foot lengths of lofting pole and to show the decoy near the top of the willows I need all the lengths, totalling therefore seventy-two feet (22 m).

As the whole area is basically flat there is no way of using the topography to show good pheasants. However, when flown over the tops of the willows they can make very sporting shooting especially as the guns are often placed in the trees with only small windows between the trees through which to shoot.

No woodland stands still and, as the life of a willow is comparatively short, a willow woodland develops, matures and declines in less than the life span of a man; the advantages of fast growth also mean a lot of work at various stages, as some trees around ponds may need regular pollarding or felling to prevent them falling over or covering the water area. It is interesting to notice that willows will always lean towards water whether a river, stream or pond – they are drawn to the water even against a prevailing wind. They are trees of great natural beauty as light sparkles on the silver underleaf of the foliage in a breeze or in the evening when the golden light filters through to make a glowing silhouette, enhanced further if reflected in the

From a painting by W.G. 'Sunlight on reeds beside the Lodge Lake'.

water below. It is a tree synonymous with water in its landscape and the one complements the other. Whilst not wanting to stray into my world as a river painter, it is not only the artistic eye that notices and is moved by such things. Most sportsmen derive much of the pleasure of the day from the beauty around them and the effects of light, which brings the landscape to life. This is the same for coarse fishermen or courser, fly fisher or ferreter, all who pursue fur, feather or fin. Those who do not appreciate such things are denied so much. A letter from a friend thanking me for a day's shooting at Hauxton said nothing of the sport itself, but waxed lyrical about the peace and beauty as he sat on his shooting stick in an autumnal glade where the sunlight dappled through the willows to catch the silver stem of a birch and the scarlet berries of the guelder rose. He probably had little, if any, birds at which to shoot but his joy was obvious and genuine and it meant a lot to me that he shared that experience in his letter. Maybe we are all a bit sentimental but feel deeply for the environment and most sportsmen are far from the hard, ruthless killers that the antis would mistakenly depict us.

Another way to improve the sporting qualities of pheasants, other than snap shooting in a glade, is to plant poplars behind the line of guns on a drive where

The poplars behind the guns on the Horseshoe Lake are now about eighty feet (25m) tall.

pheasants fly across open ground. Some of the best drives I know are not those with tall trees in front of the guns but those where the birds are making to clear the tops of trees behind. If these are on a hill then this is even more effective. Poplars grow tall very fast and in ten to fifteen years can make a poor drive into a good one and in twenty or more years an excellent one. That might seem a long time to wait but how many shoots do you know where certain drives have shown moderate birds not only for ten or fifteen years, but probably since our grandfathers' time? So think positively for tomorrow's guns; consider the good drives we enjoy today, with trees behind the guns and think of the man with vision who went out and planted those trees years ago.

So much of Britain's finest landscape and woods were planted in the past and maintained over the years by generations enthusiastic about country sports. Wise forebears took a long-term view of the countryside of which we are the beneficiaries and it is our duty not only to be custodians of that landscape, but also to plan and plant for the future. In a world where we have become so accustomed to instant results the long term future is so important. Over the centuries the activities and fashions of sports have changed. In medieval, Elizabethan and Stuart times feathered game was taken by hawking and only in the last one hundred years with the advent of the breechloader has driven game shooting been practical. The common factor throughout history is the necessity for the suitable habitat for game to thrive. The method of its sporting capture in the past, present and I trust future is dependent on the equipment and fashion at the time.

Sportsmen of the past thousand years would never have believed that any twenty-first century man could be so unnatural as to object to the taking of game by sporting methods. The threat politically is greater today than the threat to the habitat supporting game. The numerical imbalance of urban to rural population means a large proportion of the community have not had the opportunity to understand the balance of the countryside. I feel that all who care for the countryside must play an active part not just to protect country sports, but also to promote the role of sport in the working countryside by example, education and by support of the relevant organisations working for us. Maybe too late for hunting, so we must focus even more to maintain other sports.

Whenever old willows fall as the burden of ivy or rot in the trunk cause the tree to become weak and succumb to a gale, it gives the opportunity to plant other species in the gaps. If the ground is dry enough then a group of Norway spruce and oak will establish. Spruce are favourite roosting trees for pheasants and are a rich food source for the smallest of our native birds, the goldcrest; usually its high pitched *zee, zee, zee* is heard before the bird is seen twiddling up, over and round a branch above. These groups of spruce are a complement to the open willows surrounding them and are a nurse crop to draw up the young oaks which will hopefully be standing long after the spruce are gone. The oak can tolerate and thrive in much wetter soil conditions than most trees apart from willows, alders and poplars (and supports more species of insect than any other British tree as well as acorns beloved by pheasants and pigeons). It is a species which has such a history and any oak woods have a great sense of permanence. The largest oak at Hauxton is a self-set tree and one of the surprisingly few self-seeded oak trees there. It is about thirty feet (9 m) tall now and whilst not in a prominent position is the location for a straw feed around its base. On one dry mound beeches were planted four or five years ago and are thriving and will give a variety to that area. Few places are dry enough for beech at Hauxton or I would have planted more, though their dense leaves allow little light to support undergrowth.

A wise and observant keeper and countryman was Angus Nudds a friend for many years, until called to the eternal game larder. He was a man from whom I've learned a great deal. I picked his brain on many occasions or observed details of the way he looked after pheasants in the woods at Tetworth. Incidentally, I had the pleasure of illustrating a fascinating and most successful book, *The Woods Belong to Me*, an autobiography of his life in keepering since his boyhood days as a fisherman's son in North Norfolk. Anyway he once said that if he were to plant a covert for pheasants it would contain a large proportion of Norway spruce (the Christmas tree) and white thorn, for these are two of the favourite species of tree for roosting. I therefore have always welcomed self-seeded thorns as a friend and these have indeed proved very popular roosting. With his sense of humour one couldn't believe all Angus' stories or what he told you, but he was right about the spruce and thorn, at least I believed him and so do the pheasants, judging by the droppings on the ground beneath!

Home Sweet Home – Planting and Management of Trees and Shrubs for a Pheasant Release Pen

In the great clearing, one leg of the H shape was suited to the planting of trees and shrubs for a possible future site of a release pen. It was central to the shoot and would become the heart of that area and from it birds could be fed out into the other surrounding coverts and driven back home to the middle.

In Spring 1972 John and Harold, the two lorry drivers from the original gravel company, helped me one Sunday morning to plant an area with mixed conifers. These were Lawson Cypress, *Thuja plicata*, the Western red cedar, Scots pine and Norway spruce and were two year old transplants about fifteen to eighteen inches (approx 40 cm) tall. The mixture of species was a trial to see which would grow best on the area of reclaimed gravely soil which would, in winter, have a high water table. Over the years it has been apparent that the Scots pine is the fastest growing and most tolerant of damp ground as long as it is not waterlogged. In fact one end of the area planted was under water in a wet winter and all the trees died. On surrounding wet but not waterlogged ground all the *Thuja*, spruce and Lawsons died but the pines survived. On the mainly dry remaining ground all species flourished but the pines grew fastest, the spruce was second, *Thuja* third and Lawson the slowest. This was useful information for the future.

The trees were planted at a close spacing, roughly three feet (90 cm) apart as if for a Christmas tree crop. The reason for such close spacing was that I wanted a thick roosting stand of conifers and anticipated some planting losses and the possibility of one or more of the trial species not thriving. Transplants were cheap at that size and it was always possible to thin in the future. In fact this policy worked well and with gaps and some thinning, after ten years the trees were about fifteen feet (5 m) high and certainly suitable for pheasants to roost in their branches.

The dense conifer roosting was only planted on about one third of the area intended for a future release pen, in this case on the western side. Ideally the thick, warm conifer roosting of a pen should be on the northern side, allowing sunshine in all day on the southern side. The pen therefore is very light and sunny in the morning. Many people site release pens in woods that are too dark overall as pheasants really need open space where the sun can penetrate. This for young birds is as important as cover and on a fine morning after a wet night, all the poults will be out of the cover warming and drying themselves in the sun. Therefore a release pen needs three forms of habitat: thick roosting preferably on the north side, low scrub in the middle and open grass on the southern side, open to the sun with the minimum of shade. In practice, it is not as clinical as that but more varied.

In the middle shrub and scrub area any shrubs that like the soil conditions will be suitable. There is far too much concern about shrubs and berries for pheasants as whilst they will certainly eat berries, usually the thrushes and blackbirds have eaten them all long before pheasants ever think of it. The promotion and suggestion of some berried trees and shrubs will be more attractive to the owner than the pheasants, in the same way that some pretty fishing flies catch more fishermen than fish! If I was to plant any tree for its fruit for game it would be an apple. In fact a variety of apples on the edge of game coverts would mean the fruit would fall and rot or get frosted at different times of the autumn and winter. Pheasants both love to eat and roost in fruit trees. A friend, when consultant to a major East Anglian estate

designing game coverts, advised an eating apple tree at the end of each drive – not for the pheasants but for the beaters! How thoughtful, it is a brilliant idea for both.

Ten years ago there was a particularly heavy apple crop and as many of the gardens of my seventy neighbours surrounding the shoot had a few apple trees I found many of my pheasants were drawn away from home to eat them. To counteract this I got the beaters to bring boxes of windfalls from their gardens on each shooting day and I spread these strategically around the shoot. I also, for the long term, planted fifty-five apple trees of eleven different varieties in glades and odd corners all over the shoot. These are now beginning to crop and over the winter produce food for not only the pheasants but many birds.

The important thing is variety and any game covert will be more attractive with trees and shrubs of different species. I have so often noticed how contented pheasants are pottering about in gardens. The variety of shrubberies, herbaceous borders, vegetable garden and orchard, is paradise for a bird of the woodland edge. They will often tolerate barking Jack Russells and prowling cats from the house rather than reside in the surrounding woods.

Every year the release pen needs not only attention to the surrounding wire but careful thought as to how the balance of light and shade, cover and roosting all relate. Each summer before the poults are due to arrive, my friend and right hand man, Brian, and I scythe the nettles and low vegetation in selected open areas and cut some of the shrubs back and if necessary fell a tree here and there.

On a small scale this attention to detail is important and contributes greatly to the success of the season at the critical stage, when poults are released at six to seven weeks old. If they do not thrive or worse, die at this stage, they can never produce sport for anyone however well everything is done consequently. Rather in the way every flower and plant can be cherished in a small cottage garden, so on the small shoot or reserve can every shrub, tree and tuft of sedge be managed. 'Gardening for Game' was my title of the first Game Conservancy course held at Hauxton and the philosophy is still as appropriate now as it was then.

3 · The Arable and Open Ground

In the previous chapter on the woodland story, there was frequent reference to the glades and clearings. Because the management between the cover of woodland and the open areas is so closely related and important for pheasants, and wildlife, it is not possible to contain the information on only one area in each chapter without reference to the other as the book progresses. This, however, is the way in which the different characteristics of the countryside and the elements that form it should flow, no one form of habitat being an island in itself, disassociated from its surroundings, it is the delicate balance of one to another that is important.

The major 1971 clearing, described earlier, which was created to produce the series of surrounding woods has developed through a number of different forms of management. Initially, in September 1971 after the contractor's machines moved out, there were still many roots to remove by cultivating the ground, which brought them to the surface, and then manually picking them up and carting them off with tractor and trailer. I remember my brother, Guy, who is the academic and intellectual member of the family, spent a long day helping me. It was a backbreaking job picking up and carrying armfuls of long twisted roots to the trailer where, being rubbery, they appeared to come alive – it was like loading a trailer full of octopi, as one was heaved in another jumped out. He stuck it well and I was grateful to him for his help but that intellect has protected him from such work parties since! I'm afraid my enthusiasm for the whole development of the place over the years has meant that seldom have friends or family just enjoyed a quiet walk there with me. However innocent are my intentions, there is always a pheasant feed which needs a bale of straw humped through the woods to refurbish, hoppers to refill, a ditch to clear or a trap to check. Sisters, brother, cousins, uncles, aunts, anglers or municipal tree clients, nobody's immune from active participation. A friend, Patrick, from a big estate in Scotland, arrived to stay overnight. He'd had a long, tiring journey, but arrived at home an hour earlier than expected. Gina said I was still at Hauxton and so he drove over to find me. 'Just the chap' I said as I needed a hand to finish laying large concrete pavings as a base for a fishing hut. I've got a photograph of him, sleeves rolled up, sweeping them clean after the job was finished. He's now become an Earl, but I'm afraid even that will not protect him from a job in the future, though he's never arrived early since! I do admit my enthusiasm has often caused me to take advantage of those around me. I'm lucky still to have any friends – family are not so lucky, they are for life!

My original plan for the four acres (1.6 hectares) of clearing was that it should be cultivated and grow cereals. This would produce enough wheat or barley to feed duck or pheasants and a few tons for sale. Also, and this was very important, it would produce a stubble throughout the winter in the heart of the woodland which would be a great help to hold pheasants.

During the first winter after bulldozing the clearing the ground was cultivated further and then ploughed. The following spring I borrowed a set of disc harrows which made a good seed bed. An art school friend, Ernie, was staying at the time; he fancied his skills as tractor driver and chugged up and down on the little grey Fergy. On one edge of the clearing I had persuaded the drott drivers to leave a solitary and rather beautiful birch which stood proud of the willow woodland edge. As in the cartoon when a car driving across a hundred miles of open desert then crashes into the one solitary cactus, so Ernie managed to wrap the tractor and disc harrows

1973: The first modest harvest on the clearing.

around this lone birch tree. On the road he had a Mini-Moke at the time which he drove deftly through London's traffic, but the extra width of the harrows caused a serious misjudgement as he tried to manoeuvre between the birch and the wood. Fortunately no damage was done except to his self esteem as a driver.

For two years a modest crop of barley was grown but two problems developed. The first was that rabbits were beginning to re-establish after so many years of virtual extinction following myxomatosis. This virus caused such distress to the rabbit and almost as much for anyone seeing the poor creatures suffering with bulging eyes exuding pus. Unless humanely put out of their misery they would eventually starve to death as they blundered pitifully about, not able to see to feed or find their way back to their burrows.

However, by the early seventies the few survivors, having developed immunity to the virus, had begun to colonise the countryside again. It was said that as the virus was spread by the rabbit flea to rabbits in burrows, it was the 'bush' rabbits that lived out above ground away from the contagious fleas that survived. Whether that was true or not the survivors actually had developed an immunity and now twenty years later, in spite of rabbits being affected annually in late summer with myxomatosis, the actual percentage which die is less each year. In fact some rabbits can be seen which have suffered the affliction and survived with just scars remaining around perfectly healthy eyes. Nature is wonderfully clever at ensuring the survival of a species, in this case by developing a genetic immunity. Even though rabbits can do so much damage, they are nevertheless attractive animals and part of the countryside; crop and tree protection is costly but 'bunnies' make good sport and good eating.

So the rabbits eventually grazed too much of the young tender green corn through the summer leaving large areas with a stubble but no crop!

The second problem was that although the first two winters had had below average rainfall, as soon as a normal winter's rain built up the water table, it made cultivation impossible with much of the area underwater until mid summer when it receded.

I remember getting 'set' on several occasions even in the first two drier years when the Fordson would hit a wet patch; being very sandy, the soil had no body to it when wet and it became in effect a quicksand. The spinning of wheels to try and work the tractor out of trouble would just make matters worse and turn the ground into the consistency of wet concrete. It was never easy to pull the tractor out when bellied in such conditions, and any farmer friend who came to help with his tractor had to be careful not to end up in the same predicament. I spent some bad days digging to free the wheels and jacking up the tractor on blocks of wood, working in the slop and mud.

In spite of these problems I experienced great pleasure and deep satisfaction farming the few acres each year. The learning of traditional farming skills and working the land touched something deep and fundamental in me as for many who work on the land, whether farming or gardening. The smell of freshly ploughed or dug soil and the turning over the past year whilst creating a fresh start for the next brings great optimism and is good for the soul.

Watching gulls working the freshly turned soil behind the plough is a common enough sight but when I plough in an enclosed area surrounded by trees it always fascinates me how gulls are so quick to find it. There is not a gull to be seen in the sky and yet after one or two short furrows on only perhaps a two acre patch, the first gull is there, having appeared magically, conjured out of the clear sky. On the return furrow there's another and so at each turn of the tractor on the headland yet another gull is there. How do they communicate the instant a food source appears? Maybe there are gulls always watching from a great height in the sky and as one descends, the next one a mile away comes to join the first and so the network spreads the news until there is a veritable 'picnic' of gulls squawking and fighting over the next titbit as they lift and land, leapfrogging along the fresh furrow.

Farming and gardening heightens the intensity of our awareness of seasonal changes. In the spring one watches the bare soil for the first sign of life in a seed that is sown, and then leaf by leaf as the plants develop. Just as we notice the small change in a child or loved one, sensing health or sickness, so too the slightest discoloration of a leaf or wilt of a stem will signify some requirement of the cherished crop. Time stands still as we watch plants growing and yet there never seems enough time to catch up with the work they entail. As in all life, nature never stands still. First growing up, then flowering in maturity and then declining after seeding.

Yes, I enjoy farming on this small scale – so small that I must be the only farmer not to be inundated with 'freebie' agricultural magazines on Big Farm Management.

Artificial Stubble

Cultivation was therefore abandoned and a policy of natural regeneration of willow herb, rush, sedge and grasses was encouraged. This was attractive to game in itself and late in the summer I then cut strips and patches in a three year rotation. The third which was cut high in the autumn, leaving tall stalks to produce artificial stubble, is fed with tail corn all the winter either by hand or mechanically with a fertiliser spinner.

Artificial stubble has become an important management technique and a most successful innovation. It has the advantage of leaving an area which is unsuitable for

crop cultivation as cover all the summer, a benefit for nesting game and chicks, for wild flowers and butterflies.

A three year rotation of ground in this way will produce nesting cover in the second and third year after cutting and yet not remain uncut long enough for bushes or trees to colonise which would eventually smother the area. Such is the problem on large areas of former downland when grazing by sheep is not maintained. The chalk heath flora and fauna are taken over by scrub and thorn. My artificial stubble management was a form of ecological set aside twenty years before its time, but sadly without any government subsidy.

1974: An uncultivated conservation strip on a field margin or headland provides cover for game and wildlife – thirty years ahead of its time.

Orchid Management

On the areas of artificial stubble an unexpected bonus has appeared. There have always been a few spotted orchids on the grass tracks but now the larger open areas have allowed a much wider scale colonisation of these elegant and beautiful flowers. There are four species of orchid which have been identified at Hauxton, the common spotted orchid *(Dactylorhiza fuchsii)* being most widespread and appearing every year. The bee orchid *(Ophrys apifera)* is quite the most beautiful but is infrequent. One

The bee orchid (Ophrys apifera).

In early May I strim off the golden rod to allow light into the orchids when at the rosette stage before the flower spikes appear.

year it was particularly prolific and appeared in places never seen before, its translucent green flower stems grew to ten or twelve inches (approx 30 cm) before producing the characteristic delicate pink flower with rounded lip, the colour and pattern of the rear of a small bumble bee. Never had I seen them so luxuriant as usually they appear as single small, shy plants on the most barren ground. Evolution has backfired on the bee orchid, which is unusual as its first leaves emerge in the autumn. At that time it has new fresh growth at a time when other plants are retiring for the winter. Such a delicacy is eaten by rabbits which have only been in Britain since being introduced by the Romans. For the millennia of the evolution of the bee orchid there was an advantage in some way. However this is no longer so and it could be a reason why other orchid species have been more numerous, as they do not appear until the spring. Hence the name 'common' spotted orchid rather than the 'common' bee orchid.

In the shade of damp woodland there are occasional twayblades *(Listera ovata)* with their two opposite broad oval leaves at the base of a thin stem and yellow green flowers. Not very striking compared with others of the orchid family, but with a subtle beauty nevertheless when found in their dark hiding places. An exciting discovery in the summer of 2004 was the southern marsh orchid *(Dactylorhiza praetermissa)*. Seven fine specimens appeared on the bank of the Horseshoe Lake. Some years earlier Philip Oswald had identified the hybrid between this and the common spotted orchid but now the other parent has been confirmed.

It is the common spotted orchid which has responded so prolifically to artificial stubble management. This is because the annual autumn cutting produces an open light area as if it was grazed by stock. Orchids do not like competition from fast growing early season plants. At Hauxton the strange plant which has colonised most prolifically in areas where the orchids thrive is golden rod, an escapee of surrounding gardens. Orchids would never have survived the tall dense beds of this invader but they co-exist as the orchids flower in late May and early June, before the spikes of golden rod shoot up to a height of four or five feet (approx. 1.5 m) to flower in late summer. In October the growth is cut down to a height of about nine inches (26 cm) as a stubble and in the following spring the orchids again have the opportunity to grow in the open glade.

On the strength of the success of the spotted orchid colonisation the area is being enlarged each year and there are several hundred plants in an area the size of a tennis court. In recent years further encouragement has been achieved by tip toeing with a strimmer in early May amongst the young orchids. At that stage the rosettes of leaves are established and so before the flower spike appears I strim off the young golden rod shoots which by then are about 30 cm tall. This further reduces competition and permits full flowering of orchids in the glade. Rabbits are partial to orchids and when only small patches were found I used to spread willow brushwood, the tops left from the thatchers' coppicing, over these areas. It was a trick I found to be most successful having noticed that rabbits will never eat grass growing under brushwood but will eat everything all around it. The brushwood must be dead because freshly cut twigs would attract the rabbits to strip the bark and then the orchids below may he trampled and broken even though not eaten.

The same glade a month later with the common spotted orchids in full bloom.

'The Heathy Bit'

This is an open area which has another different habitat flavour and feel to it. It is an area where the top soil must have been stripped off before gravel was to be dug, after which it was left and the ballast never extracted. It is therefore a very sandy, dry and free draining area with little humus in the soil. Only low grasses, the odd bramble and a few scraggy thorns survive. In all it covers about an acre (0.4 hectare) and one patch within that never produces growth of anything more than an inch and even this is kept grazed bare by rabbits. A surprising plant which is common there was pointed out to me by an experienced local botanist, Ken Cramp, who did an extensive botanical survey in the mid '70s, a small sedge called the glaucus sedge *(Carex flacca)*. We think of sedges as tall pointed leaved plants of damp or wet sites, and yet here on the driest ground this tiny stunted form thrives with its waxy silver grey pointed leaves. Another plant which thrives and throws up a yellow flower which the rabbits must find unpalatable, is Yellow-wort *(Blackstonia perfoliata)*. It thrives on this barren ground because it does not like competition.

The 'Heathy Bit' as we refer to it is good for nesting game in the grassy tussocks and light bramble. Butterflies of grassland, particularly common blues, browns and skippers with occasional copper and comma, are active flittering among the grasses

and hedgeside in July and August. We are very fortunate in Britain that there is so much beauty in the countryside at every season. No sooner have the spring and early summer flowers caught our eye than as they fade the butterflies, moths and late summer flowers display and bring joy to those with eyes to see and mind to notice.

As I sit painting throughout the summer beside rivers from the lush watermeadows of the Test, Itchen or Kennet to the grand rivers of Tay, Spey and Tweed in Scotland or spate rivers of the north and west Highlands, I never cease to wonder at the clever and tasteful way mother nature has arranged her flowers. The early lush spring greens of vegetation, so fresh and full of vitality, display flowers of whites and yellows – the daisy, buttercup, cowslip and kingcup, oxeye daisy, yellow iris, dandelion and cow parsley. Later these fresh spring bright greens change to the darker heavier greens of high summer, greys, veridians or browns with deep blue mauve shadows. So too the colours are arranged to compliment this background with harmonies of reds, mauves and blues. The purple loosestrife, thistles, burdock, knapweed and foxglove, vetches, agrimony and willow herbs all enhance the countryside on those hot, lazy days of summer – few days they may be but they are the ones that fortunately live on in our memories. Of course there are many species of flower which contradict this theory but the hue of colour is true to its season and almost never do colours clash in nature but rather they are enhanced by other flowers or foliage around them.

Specimen Trees

A year after purchasing the main block of land, comprising entirely the area of disused gravel pit, I negotiated to buy a triangular-shaped field adjacent to the southern boundary. This was four acres (1.6 hectares) of grass divided into two paddocks. It belonged to the same owners as the gravel pits but had not been included in the original sale as one of the directors, Bill Wisbey, lived in a house which backed onto these paddocks where his granddaughter had kept her pony Anyway after lengthy negotiation a price was agreed. With the addition of this field

I had a much simplified boundary which followed the back of the houses along the southern side with access between the houses to the road.

I felt it was the right policy to extend the area if I could afford to, whenever an opportunity arose, to simplify boundaries and increase my options by securing access points to the property from other than just the original entrance on the northern side.

What I was not sure about was the best use to which I should put this land. It was a field which had never been dug for gravel and so had normal topsoil and subsoil over gravel. It was an area too small to farm, being the only four acres of arable land I had at that time. I did not want to get involved with nursery gardening which requires precise sowing and cropping dates as this would conflict with my painting trips. However, I had to find some use with a financial return, to justify the capital expense.

It was at that time I was first making contact with the Game Conservancy and avidly reading their little green instructional booklets on all aspects of game and wildfowl management, game crops and vermin control. All very interesting indeed and there was so much good information being researched and published. I know many professional keeper friends say 'well, we've been doing it all for years' but it was a distillation of the best of keepering practices, having been subjected to a scientific analysis and then clearly and concisely committed to paper for the practical benefit of many estates, farm owners and amateur keepers like me, who are interested in game management and producing a successful shoot. However, sound advice and recipes for success from the Game Conservancy will never work without diligent, reliable and intelligent keepering.

The booklet at the time called *Forestry and Pheasants* has since been updated and is titled *Woodlands for Pheasants*. There was one sentence in the original booklet which attracted my attention and stimulated my imagination. It referred to the importance of planning wide rides in newly planted forestry as eventually, when the blocks of trees grew, the angle of visibility for standing guns is reduced and in conifers particularly, the shooting will eventually become virtually impossible. The advice continued that in the early years the wide rides left for shooting could grow an intercrop of Christmas trees or instant trees.

I had always been interested in trees and thought that through. I decided that maybe my whole field could be thought of as a ride producing an intercrop. Certainly I was not on a scale to think of forestry as such. I researched the economics of both possibilities and chose to try growing the instant trees. I reasoned that when grown in forestry rides, maybe half way up a Welsh mountain, blasted by wind and weather, the trees would be difficult to extract and expensive to transport rootballed to areas of development. Maybe grown in cosy, sheltered plantations with easy access to London, East Anglia and the Midlands, it could be treated as a high quality specialist crop rather than a by-product of forestry.

At that time we had one daughter, Jacquelyn, who was two years old and hoped for further additions to the family in the future. I had been fortunate and appreciated my private education which I'd so enjoyed and wanted to offer my children that opportunity, but on the income as an artist this was unlikely or being realistic, impossible! Therefore this tree scheme was also my form of educational investment policy – I had neither income nor capital for conventional policies but had youthful energy, a few acres, and a patient bank manager. Each year I borrowed enough to buy young trees for planting but it was a long ten years before there were any sales or cash flow. However, this did slowly develop and came on stream to coincide with the demands of educating not only Jacquelyn, but Penny and Henry who had hatched by then.

I visited nurserymen to pick their brains on the best methods of growing and London Borough tree banks where municipal councils grew their own trees on surplus land held for later development. I met contractors who specialised in the moving of large trees and looking back on it, I must have been an awful nuisance to everyone in the trade. However, they were very kind and patient with me and I've made some good friends through those early contacts.

Being young and enthusiastic I was rather like a young man falling in love, quick to see all the good points but blind to the problems! In those days many semi mature trees were being rootballed in woodland and the specification for quality of crown shape and straightness of stem was not what it is today. Now even trees are grown to British Standard specifications with BS numbers. However, it did look economically viable and an exciting project on this field and I purchased my first thousand trees with the help and advice of the Economic Forestry Group who had a large nursery in Cambridgeshire. These were six to eight foot (1.8 to 2.4 m) feathered whips of five species.

I marked the field out in carefully regimented rows with the help of my father who was always very supportive of all I've done over the years at Hauxton. He had been a rubber planter in Malaya before the war and so marking out the tree field brought back memories and called for use of his considerable experience. The grass had been topped by a friend who farmed nearby who I knew from a shoot over the hill where I used to beat, pick-up or occasionally shoot.

So, with a thousand small canes marking out the field, allowing for a roadway around two sides of the triangle and a ten yard strip for a game crop on the third, I was faced with the serious work of digging one thousand holes about eighteen inches (450 mm) cubed. I went into Cambridge and at the ironmongers selected a good quality stainless steel spade. This was expensive but I considered it a good investment for my tree growing future. I could complete one hundred holes a day but it was hard work as the uncultivated grassland was difficult to dig. With holes that size it means eight for a cubic yard of soil and therefore twelve and a half cubic yards which is over fifteen tons of soil dug each day – whew – what it was to be young! After a few days I did find

two local father and son garden contractor chaps to help. By the following year, surprise, surprise, I had invested in a second-hand hole digging augur for the grey Fergy which ever since has dug the holes at the rate of a hundred an hour; whilst being rather boring it is a joy by comparison with the first year's spade work.

A thousand eight foot (2.4 m) stakes were lined up in the holes and the trees planted by the end of March. A week later I stood in the middle of the field as a steady rain watered them in, I was soaked but smiling as I shared their joy.

It all seems a long time ago, but I became very fond of the trees and they were like children as I cared for them for ten years while they grew and developed, needing support here or corrective treatment there. Also having no training in nursery practice or silviculture, like a parent I had to learn how to look after them as they grew up. Every year more have been planted on new areas of land and there are over sixty species including maples, cherries, birches, ash, planes, alders, oaks and limes. By experimenting with different cultivation and pruning techniques, the quality of the trees has continued to improve and now even though there may be in the region of ten thousand trees through the system at any one time, I still love and enjoy them and the work as much as ever. To maintain my physical involvement with the trees it is important to contain the business to a personal one-man scale and this is possible with more part-time help.

It is a joy to me that my three children enjoy working on the trees and I have found there have always been jobs appropriate to their ages and skills – picking up

Jacquelyn on the old grey Fergy 35, collecting tree prunings.

prunings – pruning the lower branches and small trees – later learning to drive the family Fergy 35 – planting in the spring – stem pruning in the late summer. I can clearly picture Penny aged eleven or twelve with a small pair of secateurs tipping back the feathers on some two hundred newly planted four foot birch, each needed thirty or forty snips, but she worked with such delicacy and patience, shaping and carefully cutting back to an outside bud. They developed into the best block of birch of twenty to thirty foot high we've grown and have now been sold to landscape prestigious developments all over the country.

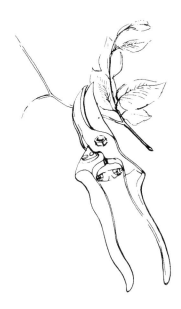

Jacquelyn will drive herself to complete legging up a block of trees for the satisfaction of seeing them with clean clear stems, though her hand is covered in blisters from the tough work with the secateurs.

Henry likewise I remember working all afternoon on a block of plane trees when he was aged about fourteen, with great patience but in a world of his own listening to his Walkman tapes. It is said that plants respond and grow well to music; it has worked not only on those trees but Henry's shot up since then as well! In his little garden at home he planted conkers every year then lined them out the following year, so seeing the whole cycle of nursery production.

In their late teens and early twenties Henry, Penny and Jackie would come home for tree pruning weekends and not only do the job very well but derive considerable satisfaction looking back at the day's work and also at the way trees they pruned in previous years have responded and developed. Ten years later their future has led them to other endeavours but their appreciation of trees and the skills required to produce a fine specimen of each species is still with them.

I have a number of friends who help now and others who have done so in the past, natural countrymen and gardeners like Harold Bushell, Len Warren and Herbie Wick, who in his eighties could still work a full day with a spade alongside men young enough to be his grandsons. One summer two friends of my daughter, Jackie, who were lady hairdressers in Cambridge, came in the evenings to remove flowers from the sorbus species, a job which is fiddly but necessary to encourage growth into the branches rather than producing berries. Once they had become accustomed to working up step ladders these two girls were so nimble with the secateurs. Flowers carpeted the ground as hair on the floor of their salon and each tree held its beautifully coiffeured head high for the rest of the summer.

A wonderful help over many years was Bob Pearson, a short, stocky fit chap who had worked on trees in the Economic Forestry Group nursery with Roy, his foreman. Both were dedicated tree men and they became good friends to me and a great help at weekends and I learned a lot from them about the finer points of pruning. Who but the conscientious Roy would come out on Christmas Eve one year to deliver

Roy is over seventy and a master pruner of trees – each one becomes a living sculpture.

trees and miss the firm's Christmas party because the roots might have got frosted over the festive season.

Bob later worked as gardener/caretaker at Ely Cathedral and spent summer weekends pruning my trees – he was very thorough yet quick and so enthusiastic. He used to sleep in a caravan by the lakes and would start at dawn to make the most of every daylight hour. One night he awoke and seeing it was light outside he jumped up and dressed, thinking he'd overslept, and with all his gear went outside only to find it was the brightness of the full moon that had woken him and it was only 2.00 am! Nationalised or privatised there aren't many in industry with an enthusiastic attitude like Bob.

In the same way that I taught Brian to prune trees, starting on small whips to cut out double leaders, tip back excessive growth, cane to straighten and thin to create a branch structure, so too he then taught his friend and neighbour, Roy. Roy is from Guyana in South America and retired from many years working for British Rail. He has so many attributes which have contributed to the success of the trees, our friendship and the spirit of the place. He is intelligent, diligent, hard-working, worldly wise and one of the most caring people in the world. He brings these qualities to pruning the trees and works often alone for hours cherishing, nurturing, correcting and encouraging them as if they were his children. He gives them love and they respond. He is at one with the world with them and has taken pruning beyond an art to become almost a spiritual experience for both them and him. I have always encouraged those I teach to treat each tree as a living sculpture and Roy has taken this to a step beyond. He is now over seventy and yet is as nimble up and down the pruning ladder as a man half his age.

For two or three years we had another member of the tree team, this was Brian's nephew, Spencer. He was a young student wanting temporary work while studying on a landscape and grounds management course. He was not only full of youthful energy which was good for us all, but was a very conscientious and tidy worker, and the different qualities of the three men complemented each other and had a profound contribution to the business and making a very happy and successful team. Spencer later was able to complete his course in the evenings and so was with us full time every day. I would have liked him to stay but he became so highly qualified that opportunities opened up in the bigger world and he is now tree officer for a London Borough. He still contributes in another role as a valued customer using the trees he originally planted and pruned at Hauxton to become landscape features in the heart of the capital. He also never misses a shooting day with his stick beating.

All who help derive satisfaction from working on trees with an emphasis on quality not quantity.

The planting parties in the spring involve a regular team but anybody new is taught that each tree is to be hand planted with loving care as if it were the one tree in their front garden. This takes a little time but soon a pattern of work develops ensuring care for each one of maybe hundreds planted in a day and consequently there are virtually no planting failures.

All trees are initially caned or staked, fertilised, weed controlled and irrigated in their early years, pruned up to four times a year and protected from deer and rabbits.

However, I have never had to spray for insects or bugs as the plantations are surrounded by natural hedgerows or woodland of the reserve which are rich in a diversity of insects and these produce balancing predators of any species detrimental to trees or foliage, which appear and devour the problem species before serious damage occurs. For over thirty years of growing trees this policy has worked but may not in a large monocultural nursery.

The physical work is a complementary contrast to my work as a painter and keeps me reasonably fit and yet artistically each tree is like a living sculpture and has the potential of great beauty. It gives me great pleasure and pride to see my trees go to landscape large prestige urban developments and bring an element of the beauty of the country into the town. As semi mature trees they are sold and moved by specialist contractors to soften the impact of large supermarkets, factories, office blocks, road schemes, airports, university colleges and private houses.

In 2004 we supplied a silver birch tree *(Betula pendula)* for a job on which Civic Trees were contracted to plant what in the *Guinness Book of Records* is the tallest tree to be transplanted in Europe. This tree was 19.7 metres tall or the equivalent of a cricket pitch in height. This was supplied with a 3 m rootball weighing 9 tonnes *(see photo)*.

The trees have never had to be advertised and having established a reputation for quality, they have sold themselves. I remember when, as a boy of eleven or twelve, I needed extra Latin coaching in the school holidays with a wise old retired schoolmaster in Cambridge. A discussion on eye-catching advertisements caused a firm comment from him in a grave tone '*Adverto* – I warn or advise', referring to the

2003: Civic Trees Ltd move from Hauxton the tallest tree ever transplanted in Europe: a silver birch 19.7m – and so earn a place in the Guinness Book of Records.

fact that the product was not good enough to sell on its own merit. Manufacturers and advertising agencies would not be head hunting the dear old Latin master with those attitudes today, except with a machete! However, he had a point and the tobacco industry have had to adopt their own bit of *adverto* by way of a health warning on every packet!

The tree crop makes an important contribution to the game. In the early stages of the crop the comparatively bare weed-free ground below is not beneficial but pheasants are happy to potter about in trees like this as to them it represents light open woodland. Later as trees reach maturity and are sold, the plantations are allowed to develop more weed growth as it is not detrimental to the crop and does produce good habitat for game. There is often a game crop or strip of permanent cover adjacent to plantations and on a shooting day pheasants are easily blanked from the plantation into the game strips where they can then be driven over the guns.

The original sixty-nine acres (28 hectares) now has small plantations on three sides as adjacent small fields or paddocks have been purchased. It is a very specialised form of land use that has worked for me economically and ecologically but it has great limitations for general use as an alternative crop or land use. There is a high initial investment in planting costs, it is a long term crop with a very limited market as the national requirement of semi mature specimen trees is satisfied by a very small annual acreage. The trees need specialist treatment and equipment and the economics are subject to the ups and downs of the construction industry and government policy at the time. In recent years the fluctuations of the value of sterling has created great competition for continental growers when the pound is high. There is not enough allegiance to British growers and trees which are best suited to our soil and climate conditions. Tree species go in fashions and it is difficult to forecast the favourite choices of landscape architects eight to fifteen years ahead.

Until ten years ago all trees sold were to contractors on a self lift basis. They had men and machines and specialised in the whole process of rootballing and transplanting. In recent times we have acquired a tree spade which is mounted on an old Trackmarshall 90 crawler tractor. These became obsolete in the farming world but are ideal for my job. We now can rootball trees in 1 m rootballs which means trees with trunks of circumferences the size of a coffee mug up to 30 cm. Large ones are still lifted by contractors but our system provides a service which makes better economic sense for my customers.

In recent years I have cut down the use of herbicide sprays by ninety-six per cent. Whereas in the past all the ground between the younger trees was sprayed with Roundup (Glyphosate), this is still used around the base of each tree and I cut round carefully with the nozzle on my knapsack sprayer in late April. This reduces competition for moisture and nutrients and in most cases the one application in the spring is sufficient. This, with trees spaced at 5 feet square (1.5 m), covers the one square foot (0.09 sq m) around the tree; the remaining ground, i.e. twenty-four sq feet (2.3 sq m) per tree, is kept weed free by rotovating. Whilst some weeds become resistant to herbicides, none can live when repeatedly rotovated through the summer. Brian loves this job and has great patience as the little tractor drones on up and down the rows of trees.

W.G. in a plantation of semi mature specimen trees.

From trial and error of growing trees over the years I can perhaps suggest a few tips and observations which apply to planting and growing trees in general whether as specimens in a garden or in woodland situations.

1   Purchase strong, healthy, stocky plants.
2   Ensure they are planted as soon as possible after lifting and if this is not possible that the roots are kept moist and frost free.
3   Ensure the ground is well prepared with any compaction or pan broken by deep cultivation or subsoiling.
4   Plant with roots spread out and well firmed with the heel of your boot. Avoid a waterlogged site – trees will grow roots down to the water table but not below it.
6   Remember trees need space and most woodland is planted too densely – trees too close together grow tall and thin.
7   Small whips need no support but larger whips or standards need caning or staking. However, these should be removed after two years. This is sufficient time for a tree to get established but before it relies on the stake for strength instead of naturally increasing its girth to support itself.
8   Trees need sufficient moisture and nutrient and therefore will establish best if kept weed free to avoid competition. This can be achieved manually, chemically or by the application of tree mats or mulch. This is the most economical way of ensuring all moisture and nutrients in the soil are available to the trees, and will minimise the need to water or feed.
9   For fine single stemmed trees in the future cut out one shoot of any double leaders annually.
10   Trees whether planted singly or as woodland blocks will require protection from rabbits and deer by guards or adequate fencing.
11   Choose and plant species you can see grow well in your area and soil type by looking at mature trees locally.

4 · Lakes and Ponds for Fish and Fowl

Construction of the Lakes and Ponds

Since the original gravel extraction, the character of Hauxton Pits is very much that of an area of water and willows. However, the fluctuation of the water table has a dramatic effect on the appearance and habitat throughout the year. In a dry summer the water area is reduced so the lakes and ponds cover only about ten (4 hectares) of the total seventy acres (29 hectares), but after a wet winter by the spring the water extends over thirty acres (12 hectares), filling the furrows left after gravel extraction and the lowest lying woodland. In spring, the small ribbons of water, shallow marsh and wetlands attract breeding pairs of mallard, Canada geese and the more recently introduced greylags, as well as other species of duck and wader on passage to northern nesting grounds.

At the time that the area of disused gravel pits were acquired there was no control of the water and any serious ambition for permanent wetlands or fisheries could not be contemplated. There were two small pits at the eastern end behind the houses in the village which I let to a small group of enthusiasts from the local Ciba-Geigy factory. This little fishery produced some good tench and bream and a lot of rudd with occasional pike in the winter.

At the western end there was a larger pit of approximately an acre and a half (0.6 hectares). This was let to a group from a government office in Cambridge, a keen syndicate who organised successful work parties to maintain the fishery. Being the agricultural department, the club's name was appropriately the Ministry of Agriculture, Fish and Food Institute of Anglers – MAFFIA, for short. A smart notice erected at the entrance ensured there were few poachers! This later merged with the Cambridge University Press Fishing Club and a successful little fishery continued until 1976.

The drought of that year, after a dry winter, brought to a head the problem of having no control of the water table; the summer water level started low and and it became desperately depleted as evaporation continued week after week during the long hot days. The water in the fishable pits was shallow and the heated water supported only low oxygen levels. The rudd and perch were the first to die and the situation was looking desperate. Up to twenty-seven herons would flight in as the sun set and take the dead and dying fish. At that stage they were doing a constructive job as the reduced volume of water could only support a smaller population of fish. Therefore some fish would have survived to repopulate if the water levels recovered.

However, the weather did not break and the water was so low that the surviving carp had their backs out of water. One afternoon, wearing just shorts and waders, I approached a pond brandishing a large landing net in one hand and a dustbin in the other to rescue the few remaining fish. I never thought how odd I must have appeared, like Neptune in the mud, until there, on the opposite bank, was a girl sunbathing naked. The surreal scenario developed as being the gentleman I am I continued to splash about catching the carp and pretending I had not noticed her– well of course I had a good look to check she was not just a figment of my imagination! Anyway she must have gathered her clothes and fled as she had vanished by the time I looked up again from my rescue mission and just the chatter of blackbirds and rasp of a jay indicated her departure through the woods. Obviously the habitat is attractive to both naturist and naturalist though no international award has been proposed for such diversity!

By mid August the fishery department from the Anglian Water Authority had netted and removed the remaining fish on the site. It became apparent that, with the original pits totally dry, there was the opportunity for machinery to clean out and enlarge the water area. Maybe the chance of a lifetime to do more – actually construct purposely designed and landscaped lakes and ponds with controllable water levels.

It was important to get some idea of the geology of the underlying strata but I could find no convincing reference in the local library. This area of Cambridgeshire has such a mixed and varied origin, underlying chalk and greensand with later glacial gravel seams over marine clays. The depth of each of these varies from location to location therefore the best solution was to get a JCB to dig a test hole. This was interesting as when starting from the bed of a dry pit, a hole was dug going through some fourteen feet (approx 5 m) of gault clay before crumbled chalk appeared when the bucket arm was at full stretch. This clay mix was definitely damp. It was exciting to find that, overnight, water rose ten feet (approx. 3 m) and so gave the possibility for a back up source of water and a spring-fed stock pond maybe for a few trout.

However, I considered it would be unwise to go through the clay in every pond or lake I might construct as I had no control over any further fluctuation of this underground water. It seemed to be better to use the clay as a base to ponds and puddle some of this up the sides to create separate clay basins. These then could be linked by pipes to each other and to the outside normal winter water table which could flow in to fill and top up the lakes. When, in the summer, the water table started to drop, the inlet pipes could be controlled to prevent the water flowing back out of the lakes. All good, children-on-the-beach, technology learned building sand castles, dams and canals to control the water of the rock pools and tide or was it all building sand castles in the air? No – I felt it could work and had a clear optimistic picture in my mind.

I contacted a contractor who arrived in early September with a D6 bulldozer and a lovely old boy called 'Fred', the driver. By then he could work on a completely dry site as the water table had dried down to the gault clay base which had been below the original gravel seam.

I had not been certain about procedures on such work but felt it was really all related to clearing out and improving an existing water area and so not a matter for consultation with the water authority or planners as there would be no significant change of use. I was reluctant to ask advice as any red tape delay could jeopardise the whole scheme for this one opportunity when time was so critical. It had to proceed immediately before rain in the autumn.

The bank manager was again contacted as another serious loan was required but an estimate was difficult. He felt therefore that it was important to visit in order to discuss this and so he arrived from Leicester. By then after a week or ten days' work, the original fishing pit had been transformed into a potential lake with what would be an attractive island in the middle. An area of willows had been felled to extend the lake area and rolled to the outside. The spoil and dry mud from the base of the pit had been bulldozed out to the edge, burying the willows and creating the banks. The sides were lined and puddled with clean clay from the base, creating a sealed basin, and then a thin layer of soil was skimmed over the clay to ensure fertility of the lake when filled with water. The surrounding banks were levelled making a track which would later be cultivated and seeded with grass.

1976: The 'before' view of the area where the Lodge Lake was constructed (the painting on the title page is the same view 'after').

It all looked rather a mess at that stage but the bank manager did appreciate that a lot had been already achieved. Whether it would make economic sense in the future he considered debatable but agreed to a loan of up to £3,000. As most of the construction sites he visited were inner city industrial developments where money disappears at an alarming rate his support was modest but patronising. However with the bulldozer and driver at six pounds an hour in 1976, the sum allocated did provide for many hours work and with enthusiasm we continued throughout October until the rains came in early November. By this time the original fishing pit was completed as a future carp fishery, another lake of about two acres (0.8 hectares) had been created from a low lying area in the middle of the site and three smaller ponds of between a quarter of an acre and half an acre (0.1 to 0.2 hectares) were made as stock ponds for the possible cultivation of carp. Another smaller pond was made in the area of the original test dig. This was deeper than the other lakes and ponds, going through the clay and so allowing the lower artesian water pressure to fill this from springs previously discovered by the test digs in the chalk below.

It was all most exciting but an ambitious project and a major development of this area of the old pits. It still looked an awful mess but even at that time, surveying these holes in the ground with just puddles in the bottom I was confident it would work. With sponsorship from Marley's, I piped through the banks at a level just above the base of each pond or lake linking one to another, sometimes with a junction when three could be linked from one central point. Other pipes went through the banks to the adjacent wet areas of the natural winter water table. This water could then be allowed to flow in and fill the new lakes and each winter provides a means of topping up. The water quality had been previously tested and found to be good and with a high pH of 8.3. This is excellent for plant, insect, invertebrate and fish growth.

Through the 1976/77 winter the lakes filled slowly and landscaping of the banks progressed and the scars of excavation receded under water. The surrounding willow woodland had been preserved, polythene bags had been tied to key trees as a guide for Fred, indicating the perimeter of the lake, as the bulldozer cleared the next section of bank These key trees remained giving immediate maturity to the landscape.

Careful consideration had been given to produce attractive wildfowl habitat on the new lakes and a large shallow shelving bay was made on what was to become

the Lodge Lake. This would be a good area to feed duck. Behind these shallows was an area of ridges and hollows where reeds were planted to create cover and shelter to enhance the ambience of the restaurant for resident and visiting duck, for hopeful inclusion in their *Good Food Guide*.

I had studied Dr Geoffrey Harrison's important pioneer studies of wildfowl habitat and Dr Mike Street of the Game Conservancy had done a lot of work on marginal vegetation most attractive to wildfowl at the ARC Gravel Pits at Great Linford. He was very helpful and we dug up hundreds of surplus plants from there to colonise the new bare banks at Hauxton.

Bur reed *(Sparganium erectum)* and sea clubrush *(Bolboschoenus maritimus)* were selected as the two plants best suited for fisheries and duck. They both produce seed heads as good food in the winter and cover in the summer. Neither grow too high to prevent fishing or are invasive into deep water and both species make a dense marginal barrier to prevent wind erosion of the banks. Other plants introduced were kingcup, yellow flag iris, figwort and great water dock to add beauty and variety but

Burr reed and sea club rush make good marginal vegetation, producing cover and food for wildfowl.

create a natural waterside environment. Existing phragmites reed on the site were used to establish the areas of taller reed beds. Roger and I spent several days planting the selected areas and they colonised very quickly making a considerable impact by the end of their first summer.

What was vitally important to the whole overall design of the lakes was that not only should they be of natural and attractive shapes but also that the blocks or strips of woodland cover in between should create new pheasant drives. This whole western part of the site had previously been so difficult to drive, being of fifteen or twenty acres (about 8 hectares) of swamp and water with a maze of fingers of willow-covered banks – wonderful habitat for wildfowl and pheasants but unmanageable on a shooting day. This development maintained significant areas of the original habitat at one end and between the new lakes and ponds which themselves produced a new open water area for wildfowl. Therefore all aspects of the sporting and wildlife interests had been significantly improved with the additional possibility of fisheries for both trout and coarse fishermen. This greater sporting potential would produce an income to justify the considerable capital expense.

It was at this time that I met a man who became a very special friend to me and to Hauxton: Carl Smith, a big strong chap who had just retired as assistant fisheries officer of the Anglian Water Authority, having worked for many years for the former Ouse River Authority. Carl was sixty-five in 1976 and had many qualities which complemented mine. His experience had been that of working for a nationalised institution where red tape, paperwork and committee decisions are not conducive to spontaneous enthusiasm or private enterprise. Therefore, he had a sobering effect on my tendency to rush at things, with positive optimism and expect immediate results. Carl and I immediately respected and liked each other and he was interested in the idea of this private enterprise and the creation of a new fishery complex. There were new lakes and ponds without fish and his advice as to stocking and setting up the fisheries was based on a lifetime's experience. We worked together making decisions and putting them into action. His friends and contacts in the authority have been of great help and his familiarity with legislation meant that the related paperwork was always competently dealt with by him. A close working relationship with friends and staff of the AWA has been successful since the fisheries started. Scientific advice, water and fish tests have been useful and later we were able to produce good quality fish from our stock ponds for angling clubs or fishery owners to whom we'd been recommended.

My earliest ambition was coming to fruition, as at the age of ten I hoped to have a fish farm. My scripture exercise book at school was filled with plans of rearing ponds and tanks interspersed with illustrations of Jesus and the miracle draft of fishes, a story which strongly appealed to me. I do not know where I got the idea as at that time (in the 1950s) there were few fish farms in Britain.

Carl taught me a lot over the years about practical fish and fishery management – which complemented the knowledge obtained from compulsive reading of books on the subject. He was receiving a remuneration as consultant and share of fish sales but this was a modest sum by comparison with his work and interest in the place. He took an active interest not only in the fisheries but as a help, on shooting days until well into his eighties and only missed one shooting day in sixteen years. He derived more pleasure and satisfaction than anything from spending a summer's day carp fishing or an evening with a fly rod on the trout lakes. He sadly died in 1998 and after twenty-two years a great loss but his memory will live on as the stones of Stonehenge survive as a monument to those men who built it.

The Trout Fishery

A fishing hut was erected on a vantage point overlooking the larger of the two lakes constructed in 1976. A mound of spoil left by the bulldozer beside the lake had a good view over the water and was in a commanding position near what was to be

A corner of the Lodge Lake.

the entrance to the fishery. I had always wanted to build a hut at Hauxton and with reclaimed timber, Georgian window frames and door, a chalet style boarded lodge appeared with long overhanging eaves.

For obvious reasons the lake became known as the Lodge Lake. A group of friends mostly who farmed or lived locally joined to make a convivial syndicate of members on a little trout fishery.

The success of this led to a more ambitious construction project when in 1979 another larger lake was made in an unproductive area to the south. This was designed again to complement the shooting and in particular to create a potentially memorable and beautiful final drive of the day, based on a horseshoe shape around which the guns could stand and have the pheasants driven from the ground behind. This has become a prolonged and complex manoeuvre, blanking birds from south and west along the back of the houses and main road to flush from the cover on the hill in the middle of the horseshoe. This lake was made when the water level was again very low at the end of the summer and one of the carp members, Peter Pratt, who had an earth moving contractor's business, arrived with his two brothers, Rick and John. They were the drivers of the enormously powerful D8 bulldozers, each machine could push ten to fifteen tons of soil at a sweep of its mighty blade. On the first day of the exciting new project the first bulldozer arrived on a low loader lorry too long to turn into the gate and so was off loaded onto the road. As the lorry went to collect the second machine forty miles away the first started work. However, a serious error of judgement took him straight into the one wet, boggy area and he was 'set', bellied in mud after only half an hour's work. Now, I would not be truthful if at that moment it had not occurred to me that they were not only Pratt by name! Things did not bode well but there was nothing to do for two hours until the second bulldozer arrived to pull him out but to go fishing! I fitted all three brothers up with rods that were kept in the shed for the children and we all four sat in the sun catching small carp on bread bait made from our sandwiches. I indicated to Peter, who was the eldest brother and 'Governor' of the business, that I had never before realised how expensive carp fishing could be, having agreed £15 an hour for each machine with driver. However Peter put my mind at rest, assuring me that there would be no charge until both his machines were working and certainly no charge for the time the first bulldozer was set, so in fact it was the most expensive fishing he had ever taken for his brothers! They reeled in two more little carp and smiled.

However, after the arrival of the second bulldozer they were fantastic, working long hours from first light until it was dark next evening. In ten days they cleared and moved 30,000 cubic metres of soil to produce a lake of nearly three acres (1.2 hectares) with half a mile of bank to fish. Regular surveying of the site was achieved with a long spirit level clamped to my painting easel in the bottom of the lake – lining up marker pegs at the anticipated future water level. A horseshoe shape was chosen for two reasons: firstly, for the attractive curve and line which is so much more natural than the straight lines of canals and reservoirs and secondly, from a practical point of view, a bulldozer could economically push soil short distances either to the outside edge or to the inside. Obviously the long outside edge will not build up high but the inside of the horseshoe where so much spoil is concentrated in the shorter edge meant that the heap of thirty feet (9 m) high was the nearest thing to a hill in Cambridgeshire. I insisted that it was not to be levelled off but left in

October 1979: The second phase of lake construction – making the Horseshoe Lake.

rough hillocks on top as high as possible. This was all later planted with mixed trees and shrubs as game cover and an elevated flushing point for pheasants driven over the lake.

The time we first drove this area was a most memorable shooting day at Hauxton. The work had been done in October and after completion the site was a muddy quagmire but pheasants and a few reared French partridges were attracted to this area, foraging for bugs and food turned up by the excavations. I fed the earth banks and rough hill at the back of the horseshoe with corn and only two or three weeks after the bulldozers had departed was the first shoot of the season. Friends were stood around the empty lake with only a puddle in the bottom. They were stuck in clay slop up to their knees; it had been too wet to level the banks. Having reached their pegs they only looked across an empty hole at a bare bank and earth mound ahead with houses and the main road behind. However, the twenty or thirty birds in the drive flew well from their muddy construction-site flushing point and produced good sport for surprised guns.

2005: Aerial view of the Horseshoe Lake having matured as a pheasant drive as well as a trout fishery.

By the following spring the lake was full of water and gave an opportunity to extend the membership of the trout fishery. In fact the economics after the capital expense of making the new lake at a cost of £3,000 meant the gross income should double and this was achieved by increasing the membership by half, from twenty to thirty, and the subscription by fifty per cent which solved the equation with a successful compromise.

The rules are simple, mostly poached from other fisheries but with various adaptations to our own requirements. Hauxton fisheries are run for friends and their friends. Rarely have rods been advertised but recruitment has been by personal recommendation which has maintained a happy atmosphere. Rules are not so much between management and members but more to ensure even, sensible and ethical fishing is maintained for all. The limit of six fish for the week, or four on any one day, allows for perhaps three visits by a retired member with plenty of time taking a brace; the busy professional man or member who travels from a distance, who only gets an opportunity to visit once a week, will have the chance (on a good day) of catching four fish.

Fly fishermen frequent the banks of the Horseshoe Lake in summer.

As a large part of the joy of fishing is the peace and tranquillity of the surroundings and communing with nature, the members are split into two groups to ensure the fishery is not overcrowded at weekends. One group fish on Sundays and Fridays, the other on Saturdays and Mondays. Tuesdays and Thursdays are open to all members and so the members of the two groups have the opportunity of meeting chums in the other half of the syndicate. Wednesday is a bye day each week when the water is rested and stocking or work on the fishery can be carried out. Therefore a member can fish a choice of up to three days out of his four allocated in a week. This looks more complicated on paper than it is in practice and it does achieve a cosy and friendly atmosphere without over fishing.

During the season a total of 1,500 trout are stocked with ten per cent brown and ninety per cent rainbow trout. The sizes are mixed to make a more natural fishery of what cannot help being an artificial form of fishing because trout cannot breed in still water conditions. Therefore sixty per cent are 1 to $1\frac{1}{2}$ lb (0.4 to 0.7 kg), thirty per cent, $1\frac{1}{2}$ to 2 lb (0.7 to 0.9 kg) and ten per cent are 2 to 4 lb (0.9 to 1.8 kg). At one time we stocked a few large trout of 6 to 8 lb (2.7 to 3.6 kg) but the result was that members

1980: A seventy foot (22m) oak bridge was constructed across the narrows of the Lodge Lake.

tackled up for the rare chance of a big trout and the normal stock sized fish were then of little sport and were being just hauled on to the bank. In any case, these large trout did not actually give a fight proportional to their size and so were in a sporting way disappointing. The optimum size for the strongest fighting fish is 3 to 5 lb (1.4 to 2.3 kg) in a still water fishery of the scale of Hauxton. It was the members themselves who suggested having more fish of the 2 to 4 lb (0.9 to 1.8 kg) size rather than the few larger fish and this is the stocking policy which has been successful for a number of years, producing good sport on light tackle.

The management of the bank-side vegetation is a delicate compromise to maintain a natural environment for game and wildlife yet allowing easy access and a tidily kept fishery. This balance is achieved by regularly mowing the grass on the top of the banks which then look attractive and cared for, producing easy walking for members and few thistles on which to catch their lines. Around the water's edge the marginal vegetation is allowed to grow wild except for selected fishing points where a strimmer maintains access. It is a fact that both on trout or coarse fisheries certain spots will be frequently fished where an area of attractive water can be covered. Such spots will develop along a bank naturally and vegetation between the popular fishing points are where the rush, reed, yellow flag iris, figwort and purple loosestrife can flourish and produce nesting habitat and shelter for wildfowl. Therefore by actually steering the angler to maintained 'swims' or fishing points the natural bank vegetation in between is preserved and ensures the minimum disturbance. In this way both anglers and wildlife are managed for mutual benefit. The angler fishes the open water unimpeded whilst reedbeds either side are a-twitter with nesting warblers and a shimmer of dragon and damselflies.

Equally important is the fact that psychologically it is beneficial for an angler to have areas of water he cannot fish as he will dream of all the big fish there just out of reach. This can either be achieved by the scale of the water which is too large to cover even by the longest cast, or it may be a length of bank with bushes and trees allowed to grow over the water's edge which physically prevents access by the angler. The latter again is not only good for the angler's imagination but for the undisturbed wildlife which populates it.

On the Lodge Lake there is a length of bank of overhanging sallows where willow warblers nest in the impenetrable brambles, which they share with wrens and dunnocks. Another length of bank has a dense bed of phragmites reed which has been allowed to develop for sedge and reed warblers to make their nests. The old

straw coloured reeds of the previous year stand waving their feathery seed heads through winter gales as mallard shelter in the lee of the wind. Then, come the spring, the same reeds stand sentinel, guarding the fresh green spikes of the new year's growth which shoot up from below the water to their full height by the time the young warblers fledge and need shelter. They live in the reed bed through the summer until they are fully grown and strong enough to fly south for thousands of miles in answer to the call of migration.

The fisherman has the joy of the chitter and churr of these warblers through the summer. These are all part of the waterside atmosphere, whether on the conscious mind of the ornithological angler, or on the subliminal of he who may not even be aware of the warbler's presence at all, but knows the sounds that surround his sport.

The Hauxton theatrical stage for the sportsman was cared for since the start by Roger Jeeves and, as I have already said, Rog was a chap who liked stability and was wary of change and so was reticent about the work proposed in the drought of 1976. True, certain parts would not be as he remembered, however with no water on the site that summer he accepted anything could be an improvement, nevertheless he watched the bulldozer every day with doubtful and wary eye.

The new lakes completed, he cheerfully took on a new role as bailiff of the fisheries – feeding fish – cutting grass – caring for members – and more important to him than anything, looking after the duck. No-one has done more over the years to help with so many aspects of all that happens on the place. We have both aged a lot since we met and a lot of water has passed under the willows, but I know neither would have wanted things any other way. He was very good at looking after the fishermen and as I'm often away painting during the summer he was always there to ensure the fishery was running smoothly – of course there are problems and being a bit of a worrier he thrived on them – he took the moans when fish are not catchable in hot weather – when an algal bloom clouded the water, or when an unsuccessful angler swore there was not a fish in the lake.

Of course with any shoot or fishery there are as many ways of running it as there are members! The policy at Hauxton is to balance the physical qualities of scale and water conditions to the requirements of members. The rules and policies are constantly being adapted and over the years I believe a successful compromise has been achieved. The fish returns were remarkable and the average for the first fifteen seasons was over ninety per cent. I wish returns like that were possible with reared game for shooting!

In recent years a number of factors have come to test still water trout fisheries in southern Britain. At Hauxton they have resulted in an average reduction of about twenty per cent on our returns. Whether it is global warming or a blip in the seasonal cycles, the overall ambient water temperature through the summer has increased by several degrees centigrade – even more degrees of the old Fahrenheit I grew up with and relate to when I dip my toe in for a swim. 70ºF or above and I jump in but below that I think twice! Now 70ºF is 21ºC and is the temperature at which trout unlike me are uncomfortable. Their metabolism slows as there is less dissolved oxygen in the water and their digestive systems become less efficient. This causes a tendency to shoal up and they then are prone to parasitic infection being in close proximity to one another. The downward spiral leads to loss of condition and at extremes fish will die. Therefore the higher water temperatures are not good for trout in comparatively shallow lakes. Big reservoirs either on farms or for national water supplies are deep and

there is always cooler water below the thermocline – that magic strata at which the warmed surface layer will not mix with the cooler water below.

To compensate for this problem I have introduced a number of new policies. Firstly, we now close the trout fishery from 15 July until 1 September. This avoids disappointment of frustrated anglers trying to catch uncatchable, non feeding fish. It means we do not therefore stock any new fish after mid June to reduce the numbers which will be subjected to stress in the warm water of mid summer. To capitalise on the cool water of spring we start much earlier and so have extended the season to optimise conditions when the trout feed, thrive and fight at their best. The season therefore now opens in early March. By bringing the main stocking of trout earlier to fulfil the exciting sport in spring and early summer the limit has been increased to five fish per day or eight in a week. Members are welcome to fish from the beginning of September until 9 October for over summered fish. Why the apparently arbitrary date of 9 October? It is my birthday and so easy for me, even if nobody else, to remember. In the interest of the wildfowl feeding policy in preparation for the shooting season it allows a month without disturbance.

Predation of trout by cormorants has also had an effect on catch returns. The enormous increase of the inland cormorant population in the last ten years has had a serious impact on many waters both still or running. They do not do as much damage at Hauxton as on some waters partly because there are only odd birds that visit and partly because anglers keep them on the move. However, they are a serious problem and I am pleased that the government through DEFRA is now addressing the situation with a more appropriate licensing system enabling an improved form of control. Cormorants are sea birds and should not be on inland waters. However, I believe it is the shortage of fish in the sea that has driven them inland where well managed waters are an easy food source.

Another threat to inland trout fisheries is a nasty little parasite called argulus, a small round jelly like creature that is now endemic in most waters. It does not often kill fish but with the warm water conditions mentioned it is another factor weakening their resistance.

In spite of these problems the sport in the four months of spring and early summer is better than ever and I have a loyal membership of the syndicate. From a practical point of view the tilting of the season's timing and stocking suits most members as there always was a much greater fishing interest in the early season and a tail off of visits from mid summer. However, from an environmental point of view nature is sending a warning that stocked trout in still waters will, if the climate warming continues, not be feasible in Southern Britain except in the deepest of lakes or reservoirs.

The Carp Fishery

This lake, as was described earlier, is of two acres (0.8 hectare) with the triangular island in the middle. The island was designed in this way to produce shelter for wildfowl in any wind condition and also as a safe nesting area for duck and geese. The carp in the lake cruise around the island feeding in the warm water of the shallows where food is abundant and the anglers on the bank can easily cast with weighted lines to these feeding fish. However, the island equally produces a limit to the distance an angler can cast as otherwise it would be possible for the modern carp angler, with fixed spool reel and weighted line, to cast right across the lake and so encroach on the water of anglers on the opposite bank. The island was therefore a positive design feature for the benefit of angler and fish as well as wildfowl.

There is a select syndicate of forty members who pay a premium subscription to fish a beautiful, private and well-managed water. They come from all walks of life and enjoy and respect the fishery. All litter is taken home and so it is appreciated as a place of natural charm. In the rules a member is allowed to fish two rods, as is customary for coarse fishing, but his wife or child can fish, using one rod each at no extra charge. This is a simple idea which encourages fathers to bring and teach their youngsters in a fishery where they will catch fish and learn to respect nature and the surroundings. It is important to encourage children to enjoy sport in the countryside for the future of the sport. Also by welcoming wives to fish or share the day with their husbands it prevents marital problems of the wife believing that the husband goes fishing as an escape from her or domestic duties. She may not come often but knows she has the choice and is welcome and this helps to maintain the happy relationship and minimises visits to RELATE for marriage guidance and maximises fun spent fishing.

It is important to encourage and educate youngsters to enjoy sport and respect the environment.

One evening each year an old friend, John Humphreys, the well-known sporting writer, who was second master at a local village college, used to bring a party of ten or a dozen boys as an end of summer term treat. These were super kids who had vied to be selected for this trip and the party usually included several who had never caught a carp before. Others who fished barren stretches of water locally were thrilled to enjoy actually fishing a water where fish abound. Some tackled up to catch a net full of small carp with float and maggot, others wheeled mighty rods cast floating crust, luncheon meat or boilies for the monsters they've heard tell of by boys in previous years. They had obviously had a pep talk prior to arrival and I gave a word of welcome and encouragement and asked them to notice how attractive the lake and banks were without litter and that I hoped they could contribute not only by taking their rubbish home that evening, but to do likewise whenever and wherever they fished. They were always well behaved and it was marvellous that they shared, enthused and helped each other in their sport. A good carp played by one could be landed by one of three neighbours waiting with a landing net! One such kind lad had his bait taken while away from his rod. The rod was towed for two circuits of the island and tangled with many lines it crossed on the way and the only solution was to swim out and rescue it. He later landed the large carp of over ten pounds along with all his pals' tackle – a most exciting battle but dreadful tangle!

As a family we all enjoy carp fishing with a summer evening picnic. Many people get a lot of pleasure fishing at Hauxton during the summer. It contributes financially and justifies the capital expense of construction and there is negligible disturbance to game or wildlife – on the contrary the lakes have contributed greatly as another form of habitat. In the winter the area is undisturbed in the shooting season when the trout fishing has ended and the carp semi-hibernate. The anglers then go to other waters where pike or other coarse fish species afford good winter sport.

Stock Ponds

The small, deep stock pond where the original test hole was made is now used to hold small numbers of trout. This makes it possible to maintain more even fishing through the season with frequent stocking of a few trout rather than an occasional heavy stocking which results in the fishing being too easy initially, followed by a famine for weeks.

The carp grown in the other stock ponds are sold at all sizes up to three or four pounds (approx 1.5 kg). The carp in the fishery produce a surplus of small fish which are removed every year to prevent the fishery being inundated and which would eventually stunt the growth of all the carp. Like the soil, water has a certain quality

An angler with a fine carp before returning it to the water.

of nutrient and condition which will control its productivity. A rich pasture will grow and sustain a greater total weight of stock than a barren hillside; in the same way a rich alkaline water will support a larger total poundage of fish. Water like land can be improved with added nutrient or lime to increase the pH. However, a fixed body of water will have a limit. By removing small fish each year the natural food in the water will then support and produce growth in the remaining fish, so the large fish can grow bigger.

For some years a successful partnership was formed with a friend, Pat Noble. We traded as Hauxton Fishery Services Limited and used the ponds at Hauxton as a base while taking on ponds and lakes all over the area on a farm partnership basis with the farmer or landowner. We produced all species of coarse fish and ornamentals suited to the water conditions. We traded these as wholesale suppliers to aquarists and the coarse fish to stock new fisheries. The success was eventually limited by our overheads which grew as fast as the turnover and the profit margin was reduced. We were making no more money with five employees and two delivery vehicles than when we started with just a boy and a van. Therefore we reverted to a small scale operation which is more fun and less worry. The smart answerphone we installed in a rusty corrugated tin shed the size of a privy in the old gravel yard, served for several years. Its message 'We regret there is nobody in the office at present to attend to your call…' had taken our orders from all over the country but Pat moved down to Devon to concentrate on the production of more profitable ornamental fish.

The stockponds are now managed more extensively and I sell a harvestable surplus annually to a local outfit who trade fish. Max and Tim who run the business are mad keen shots and so we enjoy days out together in the winter.

Crayfish

Crayfish were introduced into one pond in 1978 and have thrived in the warm water. The high calcium content is ideal and contrary to the belief that crayfish must have clear water with a stony bottom, the crayfish at Hauxton have thrived in cloudy carp ponds with a muddy clay base.

They breed prolifically and can be sold well but again marketing is a problem for the small scale producer. A cooperative was successful for some years, marketing crayfish from a number of growers but since the operation ceased trading, growers have had to sell their crop to local restaurants.

They live happily with trout and other coarse fish but I have to admit I have never yet eaten them for the simple reason that we are squeamish about popping them live into boiling water to kill them. Silly really as I enjoy eating sporting quarry I've shot or caught, but there is nothing sporting about this culinary demise of the poor crayfish.

In recent years the 'signal' crayfish *(Pacifastacus lenuisculus)*, the species I and others introduced, has proven to be a mistake environmentally. Not in the enclosed waters at Hauxton but with ponds linked to rivers it has taken over from the native British crayfish *(Austropotamobius pallipes)*. The latter suffered a great decline prior to the introduction of the signal crayfish from 'The Plague'. This has caused so many southern rivers to lose their populations. However, in those few rivers still supporting our native species they are threatened by the more dominant 'signal' – rather as the grey squirrel has from the red in so many areas.

5 · GAME MANAGEMENT

In the previous chapters I have told the story of the development and management of the various forms of habitat. It is not coincidental that such a large proportion of the book is allocated to this, as it represents the initial amount of time and effort spent on habitat improvement compared with the game itself. If the conditions are not right it is a waste of time, energy and cash to try and compensate by rearing and releasing greater numbers of game. There are many shoots which would be more successful if the annual budget allocated more to the habitat and less to the rearing programme. A high return from a smaller number of birds released into well managed woodland and cover will make more sense from a sporting, ecological economic and ethical point of view.

Vermin and Poachers – RSVP

Having established good habitat for game it is important to ensure the environment is free of predators. RSVP are not only the letters which request a reply to an invitation but also title an important priority on a shoot or reserve: RID SITE OF VERMIN AND POACHERS. Both vermin and poachers are predators of game and so are dealt with under the same heading.

   The more attractive a site is for game the more is available for opportunist predators and they will be drawn in to that food source. The honey pot effect is as true for bird sanctuaries and wildlife reserves as for shoots but strangely some reserve wardens do not practise a policy of predator control. I feel this is an irresponsible attitude as having acquired and successfully managed the habitat of a special site to attract rare species of bird they are then permitted to be persecuted by predators and breeding success is consequently reduced. In fact the same rare birds would be more likely to breed successfully next door on a well keepered shoot. It is a difficult balance to achieve but the more enlightened do resolve this successfully. The old type of warden was a keeper/warden who naturally protected the area from predation. The modern warden is better qualified in scientific knowledge but can spend too much time writing reports on why his rarities were unsuccessful in breeding because of predation rather than doing something about it. I believe the

best management is when each reserve has a keeper type warden working alongside scientific specialists who cover and report on several reserves. Both aspects of management are important and many of the County Naturalist Trusts do this very successfully.

Of course not all species of vermin are a threat to game throughout the year. The intensity of predatory pressure is focused on the nesting season. In fact wild game would prosper if the area was clear of vermin through April, May and June. If that was possible then no eggs would be lost to corvids or rats, no sitting hens to foxes and few chicks to stoats and weasels. Such would be the Utopian keeper's world. However, in practice this is not easy to achieve.

Aerial view from the south showing the present-day diversity of the area.

Rodents (rats, mice and grey squirrels) are now the only forms of vermin for which poison is necessary and is legally permitted. For generations of keepers and farmers, poisons and gin traps were the two effective weapons for control of 'undesirables'. However, the modern enlightened keeper has sufficient efficient and humane methods of control legally available to him and poisons have rightly been banned.

It is important to ensure that rodent poisoned bait points are adequately covered and protected from other animals or birds. It is advisable not to allow a build up of numbers or control is more difficult. One winter a number of rats appeared and established in a release pen where pheasants were regularly fed and it took some time to clear them as they had plenty of food other than the poisoned bait. My son Henry, who was twelve at the time, spent several evenings having sport with his air rifle shooting them as they came on to the feed ride between the pheasants.

Mice, though not a threat to game, can be a real problem in a shed where feed is stored. We had an infestation one year and so Brian and I set about them one evening each armed with a stick. We moved one sack of corn at a time and drove the mice round the shed until we'd killed all those running about before moving the next sack and disturbing another lot. By the time we had cleared the shed, no bigger than a garage, grey with dust and dirt, we had killed 222. This was a busy evening's sport and the only time we've played the numbers game and gone for a record bag at Hauxton!

Foxes are perhaps the worst threat to game. They will remove sitting hens from nests and no matter how good the weather at hatching time, nothing can replace such losses. Also reared poults later in the summer are vulnerable when first making forays out from the security of the release pen.

The fox is a wonderful animal in many ways and is so adaptable to thrive over such an enormous area of the globe. Recently as I looked down from a ski lift some 7,000 feet up in the Swiss Alps, I could see the tracks of a fox working his way round the mountain side; snow-covered for many months of the year and yet that fox could survive in the barren frozen environment. No wonder it is easy for the fox population to thrive in the lush English countryside.

The fox has produced sport for man and hounds for generations. Hunting has been an intregal and important part of country life. Now in 2005 this Labour government has outlawed it against all logical debate and the findings of its own enquiries. It is a tragedy that those living in the country are ruled undemocratically by politicians of the town. Mr Blair has no interest in the country: in fact I believe he wishes it did not exist. He does not understand it nor attempt to do so. My two grandfathers lived for hunting and will, like countless generations of country folk, no longer be resting in peace but writhing in their graves at the incredulity of today's political insensitivity and insanity. In respect of those that hunt I have not allowed foxes to be shot during a shooting day at Hauxton. All country sportsmen should thrive together and I would not wish a hunting man upset on a shooting day. The local hunt used to visit and draw the pits but unfortunately this became impossible as hounds were at risk from the proximity of roads, rail and increased urbanisation of the surrounding area.

Therefore as foxes can no longer be hunted it is important to control them by normal legal methods. Snaring is the most successful way as the tracks and footpaths make good locations for these and can be frequently checked on our daily feed round. On many larger and more open shoots lamping at night and shooting with a rifle is the most effective form of control but this is not possible at Hauxton because of the thick cover and risk to safety, as the area is surrounded by houses.

Snaring and trapping vermin is the most humane and effective method of control as traps are 'on duty' for twenty-four hours a day; obviously regular daily or in many cases twice daily visits are necessary to ensure the minimum of suffering and that they are always set.

With the proximity of many houses it is surprising that there are not more problems with cats and dogs. Fortunately neighbours look after their pets well and only the occasional feral cat is accounted for. I did once find a pair of collie dogs, one was caught in a fox wire and was sitting as if wearing a collar and lead, the other was sitting next to it. I was able to lead the one whilst the other followed and I shut them in a shed. I then telephoned to notify the police and within an hour the owner arrived to claim them – he was the local special constable – even the two dogs looked embarrassed by then!

The Fenn trap set in a tunnel is a very successful method of controlling stoats, weasels, squirrels and rats. Certain traps in key sites will consistently catch vermin, others, however attractive the position seems, will catch little. A certain amount of trial and error is necessary but once a good location is found keep a trap set there. I always have tunnel traps set next to the bin outside each release pen where the empty food bags are put. The smell of these is sufficient to draw rats and squirrels and they will be successful all winter.

Magpies and crows were rare in the early years but recently the population of both species has increased dramatically whilst the jays which were more numerous have declined at Hauxton. The Larsen trap has been the answer to the keeper's prayer for corvids, and magpies in particular are very easily caught, responding to the decoy as a challenge for territory. Magpies have decimated the population of many small birds in both town and country taking eggs or nestlings. Whilst the Larsen trap is not a new design, its reintroduction over the last few years has helped so many species of garden bird as well as game species.

A controversial issue, however, is that I think the magpie has had a considerable effect on the wood pigeon population. No bird nests with such conspicuous offer of eggs than the pigeon. The two bright white eggs are served up on a flat round nest like an 'early starter' breakfast at a Little Chef. The magpie wouldn't even need the menu. The result of this depends on your attitude to pigeons. The farmer is not thrilled at the increased pigeon population threatening his crops whilst the pigeon shooter is delighted with the prospect of more sport. As an enthusiastic pigeon shot, I therefore am of the

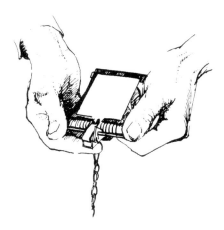

latter view but accept the responsibility to reduce pigeon numbers and protect the crops on farms where I enjoy the opportunity of shooting. In this way both farmer and pigeon shooter are happy.

Mink have occasionally been a problem. There is an alarming population on most river systems in Britain. They represent a great threat to all wildlife as nothing is safe from the top of a tree to the bottom of a river. They climb, swim and hunt with great skill and agility and must be controlled at every opportunity. They are not difficult to catch in a baited cage trap. The few I've caught at Hauxton have been caught surprisingly in traps set for fish or crayfish. Once I caught two in a crayfish trap baited with a dead rabbit, five feet down on the bed of the lake. On another occasion I caught one in a Fenn trap set for rats in a shed.

Poachers

One has some respect for natural vermin, whether of feather or fur, but not so with the two legged form. The youngster or old village character is all part of the rich pattern of the country life but organised poaching is theft and should be dealt with in the courts with the severity of burglary. Fortunately the small scale of Hauxton means that for a number of reasons, poaching is not a great problem. Firstly, the numbers of fish or fowl involved are small compared with larger shoots. Secondly, it is more easily protected with an intense set of alarms. Thirdly, it is easy to patrol, in fact from a central point one can hear everything on the whole area. Fourthly, being surrounded by houses there are many friendly eyes and ears who notify me of any strange person, noise or light. Fifthly, reared pheasants are all permanently marked which makes them easily identified and difficult to market. Finally, it is physically difficult to get about, especially at night through water, bog, thorn and thicket. The beaters find it difficult enough even when encouraged in daylight to get through the cover.

In addition, because many of the local police enjoy fishing, bird watching or beating, they always keep a personal as well as a professional eye on the place, day and night and we maintain close co-operation. On one occasion when some trout were being poached, one of the local police, Barry, used to wait for the thieves at night when he was off duty, until the three rogue vermin were caught, apprehended by three Panda cars full of police officers and two Alsatians.

While some shoot owners bemoan the low price of game in recent years, I see this as a significant disincentive to poachers. Should game be more valuable the increased cost of additional security would far outweigh the extra income derived from the higher price of game on all but the largest shoots.

Pheasants

In the first few seasons we shot a number of wild pheasants in modest bags of very varied species. With such mixed habitat it is this variety of quarry rather than the numbers which have always been a feature of sport at Hauxton.

By 1973 the potential was there for the shoot to escalate having opened up the woodland and improved the cover. In fact it was a good friend, the late Jeremy Glyn, who had a fine shoot and estate at Albury in Hertfordshire, who phoned one day to say his keeper, Jim, had two hundred pheasant poults surplus and would I like them for Hauxton. What a kind offer and also a new keepering challenge and I was thrilled and grateful to accept. I had just won a hundred pounds in the Cambridgeshire Hunt supporters' draw. How better to spend it than to construct a release pen to protect the pheasant poults from the foxes. I reasoned this an appropriate use of this prize for the co-operation of sports relating to foxes and pheasants.

I followed the Game Conservancy design for the building of a release pen, as they had distilled a successful recipe for this and the management of released poults. It was a wire pen six feet (1.8 m) high with a foot (30 cm) of wire turned out and pegged at the base and another foot (30 cm) turned out at the top. Therefore a minimum of eight foot (2.4 m) of wire is required to keep out 'Charlie' the fox. Pop holes with fox proof grills were inserted at about twenty yard / metre intervals around the perimeter to allow the poults re-entry, having flown out free winged. However, initially the outer primary feathers are clipped on one wing to prevent premature escape. This holds them in the pen for two to three weeks while they become accustomed to the area as home and where food is always available by hand and hopper feeding.

Certainly we had good sport and Jeremy came on each day's shooting. His generosity did not end with the production of the pheasants, he brought two chaps, Peter and Phil, with dogs to help beat. We shot four days that season and on 4 December set a great record with the first day of over fifty head of game. One gun, Jonty Galbraith, a farmer friend from Dumfriesshire down for the Smithfield show, nearly missed it as he'd left his gun and Wellington boots in the Brompton Grill the night before! Even these days an absent minded character like Jonty would be unlikely to be mistaken for a terrorist.

Jeremy's kind offer of poults appeared again the following season and it was only when it occurred for a third season that the truth of his generosity was exposed as in fact he'd previously asked his keeper to actually rear an extra two hundred for me, they were not 'surplus' as he'd suggested.

As the cover has developed further and my knowledge of keepering and pheasants has been extended by experience and by picking the brains of helpful keeper friends everywhere, the shoot has continued to expand and build up. This would not have been possible without a lot of help from others as regular feeding is so vital for the weeks after release and over the years there have been a number of key people. Ken Moss was a short, round man with a constant smile who had worked for twenty years or more for the Gravel Company. I had allowed the company to still trade gravel from the yard for a period after I purchased the site, as while I was away at art school it was helpful to have someone about. They brought in ballast sand and shingle by the lorry load and sold it in small quantities to jobbing builders and farmers locally. I continued this later in a firm which I set up; the Hauxton Sand and Gravel Company, in retrospect rather an imposing name for the bucket and spade operation it was. Ken (the 'boy') then worked for me continuing to serve the sand and gravel to customers and also helped to feed the pheasants when I was away. This worked well for a few years until Ken's health deteriorated and he retired and died when only in his early fifties. It was a sad loss but he was an example of a man who did not need education or wealth to bring him happiness. He was one of the most contented and cheerful chaps I've ever known.

Life has a wonderful way of producing the right people at the right time and the gap was soon filled by Lindsay who was a local policeman. He had helped Den Northrop, a friend who farmed over the hill, with his shoot and lived in Hauxton. As Den used to help with his friend Roy on all shooting days in the early years, I had known Lindsay for some time. He's a chap with a wonderful and at times wicked sense of humour, always cheerful and the joker in the pack of beaters. He was always resourceful at manipulating his duty shifts so that he could feed the pheasants at the right time.

I had always anticipated an amateur minus factor with our keepering but in fact I soon found that, to the contrary, conscientious enthusiasm has in fact compensated for our inexperience and consistently good sport and returns have been the dividend.

After a couple of years Lindsay retired from the police and moved away to live the other side of Cambridge and so was unable to help with the keepering. He took another job as a security officer for the local newspaper and still somehow works his shifts to help beating on shooting days. Last season he was joking with fellow beaters at the beginning of the day when he was surprised and shocked to see the owner of the newspaper group drive in the gate. He didn't actually jump to attention and salute but he came up to me to confirm that it was Lord Iliffe. 'You might have told me' he said. Later in the day I stage managed Lindsay to be a 'stop' near where Robert Iliffe stood at his peg, having primed Robert that his *Cambridge Evening News* security officer was one of my key helpers. An amusing conversation obviously took place and a pact between them agreed that neither would tell on the other 'skiving' for the day!

Once again in 1980 the gap was filled miraculously by a lovely local rogue I'd known for years, as he worked on the neighbouring farm. Brian Morley, a few years younger than me, used to come with a couple of mates, Len and Dennis, to ferret the rabbits in the pit every February. Brian is dark and swarthy, a strong chap with thick black hair that is long enough to keep his ears warm in winter and the gnats off in summer as it protrudes from below an old pork pie hat which his neighbour says he shares with his garden scarecrow. He has become a wonderful friend and is one of the most natural countrymen I know. He is very observant and has a sharp eye for all about him. However, it is hard to instil any sense of urgency into Brian but once the right day dawns for a job, he will do it well.

He first helped with the pheasants in the winter as work on the small farm was

slack and his 'Guv'nor', a great countryman and sportsman, Mark Bradford, allowed him to pop over and feed. Mark had been a member of the trout fishery since it started and helped picking up on shooting days until his knees gave way. Until over ninety, he was present every shooting day as a 'stop' and in charge of the game cart (his truck), in the back of which he hung the game. Sadly he has now gone to the celestial game larder after a long and full sporting life. Brian now is self-employed and works for me. Not only a close friend but my right hand man in helping with all the activities of keepering, trees or fisheries.

For three years with the pheasants generously provided by Jeremy, they were sexed as hatched and therefore roughly fifty/fifty cocks and hens. This modest rearing programme produced extra days shooting but a problem soon became evident. The original good stock of wild hens was being subjected to the extra shooting pressure of the additional days. By the end of a season even though the last days were cocks only, it was predominantly reared hens that survived as the wild ones, having flown best, were selected by the guns and mostly shot. Very soon therefore the wild stock of hens was replaced by poor breeding reared ones which is absolutely the opposite of what one would hope.

That fact combined with a report on research by the Game Conservancy which found that reared cock pheasants wandered less than the hens, gave me the idea of releasing only cock poults. On this mini shoot the stay at home cocks could make

Reared cock pheasants on a straw feed ride.

sense and give a better return. Also it would mean that on a shooting day the guns would be told to shoot cocks only, allowing the stock of wild hens a chance to recover.

Certainly the returns of the reared birds increased dramatically from an average of around fifty per cent from both sex release to sixty-five per cent with cocks only. Since this first experiment in 1981 the returns have remained above sixty-five per cent with most seasons being above seventy per cent and a record in the 1989/90 season of seventy-four per cent. These are percentage returns of the reared birds only, having been wing tagged. At the end of the day it is easy to check through the bag and note the results from the birds marked in this way.

In the last ten years it has been interesting to experiment with different breeds of pheasant. There was no question that previous standard mix bred birds would hold well, we had proved that. However, it was a challenge to find a breed which would hold well and maybe fly higher and faster. The American Michigan blue back certainly has the latter qualities but is a notorious wanderer. However, I tried the first cross between American x Standard English for two or three years with some degree of success. They did fly well but they also had traits of the wanderlust and so returns dropped to between fifty-five and sixty per cent. Whilst this was really quite successful and a worthwhile trade off to achieve better quality sporting birds, they were a keepering nightmare. Brian and I were constantly depressed as we saw so few birds about, the food did not go and we did not hear them 'cock-up' to roost. The place seemed devoid of pheasants and yet on a shoot day the drives produced birds as if by magic out of nowhere. We tried Scandinavian x English cross birds and they did well but the game farm only produced them as an experiment one year as fertility and therefore hatching percentages were uneconomical.

Then I saw some pheasants on a shoot in Hampshire that I liked immediately. They obviously held well and would take off and rise at a steep angle to fly over tall trees – exactly what I wanted for Hauxton. These were a strain of Black-Necked pheasants from a French stock reared in Devon. It was a long journey and they were more expensive as poults but for three seasons now they have been the most successful breed for Hauxton. They fly as well as the American Blue backs yet hold well, we see them about in the course of a keepering day and they are a big strong bird which at the end of the day makes a good meal.

The scale of release has increased and peaked between 1998 and 2001 at eight hundred poults which proved to be a successful number to provide seven driven days and two extra rough shooting marauds at the end of season. With the withdrawal of Emtryl as a disease preventative in the food I have reduced the number of poults by fifty per season for two years. This decreases the density in the pens which in turn reduces stress which is a major cause of disease in the first place. The challenge was to shoot a similar number by ever improved management. The cover would now hold and support a much greater number of pheasants but it would not be sensible, ethical or sporting to have days of big numbers. A day of around one hundred head of game of mixed species is a good day among friends on this small shoot.

There are two release pens, the oldest one with some of the original willow woodland and thorn scrub but with groups of spruce and shrubs planted for improved cover and warm roosting. The site of the second pen was planted in 1971 on a wing of the new H-shaped clearing in the original woodland and was planned to make a release pen in future years. This took ten years to mature sufficiently to be an attractive habitat for a pen with a good balance of open ground, scrub cover and roosting.

Each pen is visited twice a day to check that all is well and fed by hand as well as hoppers. The pellets are fed in many containers on a path within the pen. These may be old frying pans, Fray Bentos steak tins or whatever, but by placing the pellets in these it prevents the food coming into contact with wet ground which is wasteful. Each feed dish has a makeshift shelter of tin or asbestos to protect the pellets from the rain. These numerous feed points, which are situated every ten yards along the feed circuit, have the advantage of separating the young pheasants into small groups like broods rather than being in a concentrated flock along a feed ride. This helps prevent tail pulling, a great problem with poults at about twelve weeks old. On most shoots this is an inevitable problem but we seldom have pheasants suffer a delay to maturity in this way. There are three positive solutions which I believe help to avoid tail picking: firstly, as explained, the feed is dispersed to encourage brood size groups; secondly, the continuation of a high protein pellet diet rather than weaning them on to wheat at an age when they still require extra protein for growth. Wheat is introduced to their diet at about twelve to fourteen weeks old but only at twenty per cent. The percentage increases until they are on ninety per cent by November, when they are fully grown with good tails. A nominal ten per cent pellets is a good holding addition to the diet for a week or two longer. Thirdly, the release pens are large for the number of poults released and so they have sufficient space. Probably the two main causes of tail pulling are overcrowding and lack of protein. Certainly if extra protein is then not provided it takes a very long time for pheasants to regrow tails and too frequently on some shoots they are still 'bob tailed' on early shooting days.

As Emtryl had been incorporated in the feed pellets as a prophylactic prior to its withdrawal in 2002, it was important to address the increased possibility of disease and the following five steps have been taken.

1   Reduction of stocking density referred to earlier.
2   The introduction of automatic bell drinkers to replace the previous plastic window box with ballcock system. These were open topped which meant birds could perch on the side and if turned round would defecate into the water with the potential for contamination and disease. The bell type drinkers have a narrow trough surrounding the base of the drinker which is raised off the ground and not possible for birds to perch on and so the water is always clean. In addition each drinker has a plastic mesh stand below them and so the birds have to stand on this which prevents contact with wet ground or faeces. The header tank and system is all flushed through and sterilized before the birds arrive.
3   The feeding system has been changed from open feed tins on the ground to

enclosed hoppers which prevent faeces contamination as was achieved by introducing a clean water system.

4   A powder called Probiotic is added to the water – four days on, four days off. This is a natural bioculture which, like yoghurt, stimulates beneficial bacteria in the gut and boosts the enzymes in the digestive system. This then enables optimum use of nutrients in the diet which in turn heightens the resistance to disease.

5 (a) To prevent an outbreak of coccidiosis the birds have a course of Baycox in two applications firstly twenty-one days after arrival and then again twenty-one days later.

  (b) To prevent parasitic problems we apply Panacure ten days after arrival. This may be necessary again later if signs of 'gapes' are evident.

These actions have proved successful for the past two seasons since implementation, in fact the poults have been more healthy and with virtually no in-pen mortalities so far – touch wood!

On the small shoot with amateur keepering I recommend releasing late pheasant poults around mid July at seven weeks old. These only take keepering time in late summer and the birds have less time to stray off the shoot. Feed high protein pellets which will bring the birds to maturity two weeks earlier than if fed on wheat prematurely. I believe this policy will produce a better return with less work and will more than compensate for the additional feed cost.

To avoid the reared pheasants becoming too tame, for the last two years we do not whistle them up at feed time. We have found that the regular feeding is sufficient draw to hold the birds and this policy encourages the pheasants to become more 'wild'.

It is important that pheasants should always have water available and they drink more than one would imagine. In dry weather we find a gallon of water will be consumed by thirty poults each day.

On every visit to the pen we walk round the outside to check fox wires and walk any poults that have flown out round to the next pop hole where a wing of wire mesh leads them in. This frequent shepherding manoeuvre helps train the birds to re-enter the pen on their own and is important to help the young pheasants return home to safety, food and water.

As September turns to October, we start what we call the 'inner circle' feed rides. These are straw feeds in woodland around the pen area, then later in October we start to feed the pheasants into the outer woods in preparation for the drives on shooting days. They will then fly well over the guns when driven from the outer woodland back home to the middle of the shoot.

In every glade and sunny corner there are dusting shelters, feed hoppers or a branch nailed across two posts for pheasants to perch in the sun. All these toys are intended to entertain the pheasants and prevent them from wandering. A pheasant likes to walk about all day and so I make the woods like a pheasant's amusement park. A piece of plastic binder twine from a straw bale, if tied to a branch so the ends hang just above the ground, will entertain a pheasant for hours as it pulls it into shreds. It all sounds silly perhaps, but to hold pheasants on a small shoot when no boundary is more than 300 yards/metres from the centre takes a certain ingenuity.

The contribution of wild pheasants to the total season's bag is not great as the acreage is so small. Over the years an average of around thirty wild cocks are accounted for and assuming that there are as many hens this would mean a production of approximately one wild bird per acre. This scaled up would equate to the great wild shoots of the past when, for example, Elvedon or Holkham would produce bags of twenty to thirty thousand wild pheasant a season on as many acres. The wild pheasant and partridge management is still successfully maintained on a number of shoots I know in East Anglia and they have shown modern farming and wild game can co-exist but these are exceptions to the rule. However with the new

A covered feed shelter where food is still available after heavy snow: for the rest of the year it is a dusting shelter.

agri-environmental schemes there is a real opportunity and encouragement for wild game management.

Therefore at Hauxton the few wild birds in the bag are an achievement but having said that, the disappointing fact is that in spite of not having shot hens for some years, the numbers did not build up. By the end of the winter the numbers remained remarkably constant with thirty to forty following good or bad breeding summers. However this may have been due to a dispersal factor which would help populate the surrounding area rather than create a shootable surplus on my few acres.

I have great respect for all wild game. For Mrs Pheasant and Partridge to nest successfully and produce a harvestable surplus, all keeping and farming policies have to be positive and even then all is at the mercy of the weather conditions which are so critical, particularly in the first week of a chick's life.

I am continuing my reared 'cocks only' stocking policy in spite of only modest success from the wild birds. This, together with the proven success of the fifteen per cent better return from reared cock poults, is sufficiently good reason on this small scale. However, since the expansion of a friend's shoot on the hill to the East we have had a number of visiting tame hens. This unfortunately means my hens are now not solely a wild stock. However, I have conducted my experiment for long enough over twenty-five years to realise the limitations of scale. It was important to enjoy doing that but little point in cherishing reared hens which were not likely to contribute successful broods. Therefore we shoot both hens and cocks on most days now. This still leaves the same number of hens in the spring but sadly no longer a true wild stock.

Partridges

Partridges require more open habitat than that at Hauxton. However, every spring a number of pairs of both English and French partridge come in to nest. These are often successful but then they take their broods back out to the surrounding farm land and so do not contribute to sport on shooting days. However, to provide safe nesting sites and broods which populate the surrounding area is very pleasing.

In 1979 and 1980 I tried releasing one hundred Chukar x French partridges. The Chukar is more at home in scrub cover and they did hold reasonably well in spite of the small acreage of the shoot. A return of around forty per cent was achieved but the disappointing fact was that those which stayed became too tame and were an embarrassment on shooting days running about between the guns and seldom making sporting shots. They did not breed successfully in spite of making a nest and incubating their eggs. The broods when hatched soon dwindled and none survived. I believe this hybrid has contaminated the wild stock of French partridges by interbreeding; 1992 was the last summer the crosses were allowed to be released. The good news is that the pure Red Legged partridge stock has renaturalised with better breeding success and a greatly improved sporting quality.

Mallard

Initially winter feeding for evening flighting was tried. However, this was not very successful, probably because there was no large 'bank' of duck on which to draw in this area. As the fens and washes in the north of the county are so attractive, it is not surprising that the winter wildfowl population all stay there, resting on the dykes and open water during the day and flighting to feed on stubble or potato fenland at night.

Many pairs come to nest at Hauxton in the spring. However, for two reasons the actual breeding success is limited. Firstly, because gravel pit areas are not fertile and rich in insect life and secondly, the broods hatch early in the spring before there is sufficient insect life at all. Therefore as ducklings must have a high protein, insectivorous diet in their first weeks many do not survive. The problem is compounded in the lakes and ponds stocked with fish which themselves reduce the insect population significantly to the detriment of young duck.

To solve this all the eggs found before 31 March were collected and Brian and his father, Bert, kept these in an incubator on the sideboard in their sitting room where the ducklings hatched. The next stage was a small pen made of cardboard boxes on the floor, where the day old ducklings nestled against hot water bottles. As Brian and Bert lived alone there were no women in the house to complain and this domestic rearing scheme worked well. Later the lawn was covered with wire pens and finally they were reared to six or seven weeks old down at the farm.

Eggs were hatched and ducklings reared in Brian's living room.

Since Bert died, Brian has moved to a smaller house but the principles of the duck rearing are much the same.

At around seven weeks old they are introduced to a release pen beside a pond. Mallard release and feeding is easy and a small pen will suffice as after only a few days half can be let out. Those inside want to get out but those outside peck at the wire and are as anxious to get in! In this way we rear and release in the region of 150 mallard each season.

As duck are such gluttons they hold close to wherever they are fed. In fact this can be a problem with reared mallard as they become too tame. If ad lib hopper feeding can be used they will be more wild and so we feed at different places on the lakes to get the duck used to flying from one to another. We try new tricks each year and

Mallard are released from pond side pens.

usually mallard make most exciting shooting, flying high or fast and acrobatic in a wind, equally they can be heavy, slow and make disappointing sport on still,windless days.

We do not have a duck drive as such and guns are given strict rules, being allowed to shoot five duck or seven shots whichever comes the sooner! Duck may fly at any stage of the day but usually more are seen in the afternoon when we do the pheasant drives around the lakes. In this way guns select duck of a sporting height, shoot, mark and pick up all birds down and so have some variety of shooting during the pheasant drives. About twenty or thirty are in the bag each shoot and these are a popular choice when offered to the guns at the end of the day.

The wild duck from which the early eggs were collected nest again and hatch

Mallard raid a pheasant hopper – but who can blame them!

when the weather is warmer and there are more insects about. These wild second broods very often do well and augment the reared duck.

The management of duck in this way can be remarkably productive. As an example, in 1978 we monitored five duck from which fifty-eight eggs were collected. From these forty-eight mallard were reared and the second broods produced an additional thirty-six. Therefore more than eighty young were produced from the five pairs. However, sadly it is rarely as successful as that!

Other species of duck are occasional visitors including pochard, teal, gadwall and pintail. Tufted duck with their smart heraldic, black and white plumage, nest and usually breed successfully on the fishery lakes. Being diving duck they thrive in deeper water than mallard, which like to dabble in the shallows.

Geese

Originally there was a large flock of over one hundred Canada geese. This was an unacceptable number on the area and produced considerable damage on local farms. The numbers are controlled by shooting to maintain between twenty and thirty. Their 'honking' as they fly over the village from the watermeadows to the pits is an evocative sound and welcomed by the residents of Hauxton as a sound of the wild as they look up at the skeins passing overhead. Greylags are a more attractive and natural bird and I introduced these in the early 1980s. They have now colonised successfully and their broods are large with eights or nines compared with the Canadas usual five to seven goslings. Foxes will take geese eggs but having hatched it is rare for all the brood not to survive. They suffer no predation and thrive on a vegetarian diet which is more dependable than are insects for young duck.

Whilst inland geese are hardly the sporting quarry of the hardened coastal wildfowler they do produce memorable shots. Late in the season we flight them at the end of a winter afternoon and everyone remembers their first goose. I remember well when aged sixteen my son, Henry, was all smiles as he carried his first back to the yard. 'They're quite heavy aren't they Dad?' was his observation after two hundred yards!

Woodcock and Snipe

The open and coppiced willow woodland is ideal habitat for woodcock and they offer very sporting shots and variety on a shoot day. However, as they are on migration they are seldom visitors for more than a day or two. Usually there are one or two in the bag each day; on one of the first ever days at Hauxton when the bag totalled eleven pheasants there were thirteen woodcock. Needless to say the legendary pigeon shot, Archie Coats, accounted for seven of those. Some estates do not allow woodcock to be shot but I personally do not believe shooting has any significant effect on their population which is much more dependent on conditions relating to the favourability of annual nesting, migration and winter feeding. However, I respect the views of others and keep a very open view on the subject. In the meantime it is a welcome visitor, a sporting quarry and a tasty delicacy for supper on a winter evening.

Snipe and woodcock used to be much more numerous at Hauxton before the watermeadows by the river, beyond the church, were drained in 1986. Prior to that time they would rest by day in the old gravel pits and flight to feed on the rich, marshy meadows by night. It is not sufficient to still have the good habitat for daytime resting if the feed grounds have deteriorated. Sadly this has happened all over Britain where extensive drainage schemes in the last twenty years have greatly reduced the acreage of boggy areas favoured by snipe.

In 1987 the original woodland clearing was developed into an area of scrapes. The fishery lakes had produced deeper water areas but there were few shallow open areas of water. To encourage wildfowl and waders which require shallow marsh or sandy beaches and spits, I designed this two acre (0.8 hectare) scrape area. A bog tracked bulldozer achieved this easily at the end of the summer, making depressions with intermediate ridges. These depressions were of different depths so that whatever the height of the water table there would be shallow flashes of water available. Even in years of drought the deepest scrapes still have sufficient water in the bottom and the multitude of bird and animal tracks in the muddy margins show just how welcome those water holes are. Visitors to the new scrapes include the

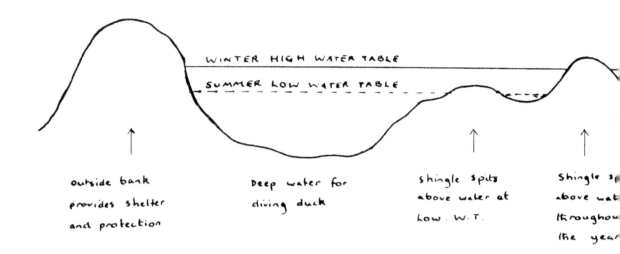

outside bank
provides shelter
and protection

Deep water for
diving duck

shingle spits
above water at
Low. W.T.

Shingle s[
above wat[
throughou[
the year

Bulldozer constructing the scrape area in 1987.

Diagram of scrapes area showing the stepped levels to produce
shallows for waders and dabbling duck at any water level.

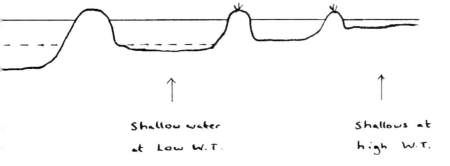

Shallow water
at Low W.T.

Shallows at
high W.T.

A promontory was covered with polythene to prevent weed growth, before being topped with gravel.

common and green sandpiper, the little ringed plover, snipe and water rail as well as various species of duck. The appearance of the scrape is similar to that of fresh gravel workings and it will require future work to prevent the area colonising and growing over with willow and scrub.

Pigeons

The wood pigeon, though it is agriculture's number one bird pest, is my prime sporting quarry. No other bird produces such a variety of sporting shots. It flies high, fast down wind, it twists and jinks when its sharp eye spots any danger and is totally wild. Therefore at Hauxton it receives a lot of respect and breeds successfully in the sanctuary of the keepered woodland.

Whilst I enjoy inviting friends and guests to shoot the game on shooting days, I enjoy the pigeon shooting myself, with those who help with the keepering. Brian, who is a very good pigeon roost shot, usually joins me. We get one good afternoon flight in late September or early October in the Everglades area. This is away from the pheasant pens and in any case pheasants are not disturbed by a pigeon shooter who is shooting from one position. Frequently when decoying pigeons I have had pheasants feeding nearby on the same field, once they have established that the shooter is not on the move.

Aerial view of the scrape area with high water table the following spring.

At that time of year with a steady breeze and a lofted decoy on a pole set high in a willow, good sport can be enjoyed all afternoon and evening as the pigeon come back to the wood to rest between flights to feed. I have shot as many as fifty to eighty on such a flight, such marvellous sport and testing shooting.

Winter roost shooting in February and March is confined to a short time, just the last hour or so of the day. The woods are not regular evening pigeon roosts but used when there is food available on farms in the area. On such evenings we never get large numbers but a few sporting shots and Brian and I would account for perhaps fifteen to thirty birds between us.

With no farm cropping on the shoot there is no decoying possibility, but I do get good days decoying locally of pigeons coming on a flight line from the Hauxton woods to stubbles in the autumn. In this way, successful summer breeding in the woods on the shoot provides me with sport elsewhere in the locality.

Rabbits

Again a pest species and a real problem at times if they get into my specimen tree plantations. However, they provide good sport with a rifle on summer evenings. Roger was a top competition small bore rifle shot when he was young and he had a powerful air rifle which he used to good effect on rabbits around the fisheries. On Wednesdays, the fishery bye day, he would kill about a hundred over the summer months all shot in the head at up to fifty or sixty yards range!

Brian and I, and when he's at home, Henry, have some good summer evenings shooting with my .22 with a sound moderator. The person shooting stands with head and shoulders through the sun roof of Brian's Daihatsu and we slowly drive round the woodland tracks stopping for shots as and when rabbits stay sitting for long enough. This form of shooting demands a strict safety discipline. We will get up to fifty on a good evening – a fine evening after a wet day is particularly good for that sport.

Brian and his mate, Len, used to enjoy ferreting the hedgerows in February as another form of sport with rabbits.

Ground game is not shot on shooting days as with 'stops' and beaters in front of the guns and people picking up usually out of sight behind, it is not safe.

It can be seen therefore that every quarry species is managed and contributes to sport throughout the year and of the total head averaging in the region of a thousand per season, approximately half is wild and half reared. Although a large proportion of the wild quarry is made up of pigeons and rabbits, they are highly valued for their sporting qualities and should not be underestimated.

6 • THE SHOOTING DAY

I seldom sleep well before a shooting day, partly with excitement but more from anxiety as I run through all the details of the organisation in my mind yet again. The professional keeper has the worry of his game, beaters, weather, etc. The shoot manager or owner will think of organising his guns but the amateur keeper on a DIY shoot has to consider and organise every aspect of a day. I am fortunate that my beater friends are a very reliable team but I dread the ring of the telephone the night before a shoot as someone has flu, a key spaniel is 'in season' or has cut its leg. Inescapable problems with health, transport, work, children or mother-in-laws to say nothing of the doubts about the weather, there are so many possible variations but amazingly there is usually the full complement of beaters, guns and pickers up, by the time we move off on the day.

I'm always being told by friends who shoot with me, how relaxed and friendly the days are at Hauxton. I decided that if everybody else is so relaxed maybe I should try it. As soon as I followed that philosophy things started to go wrong! I forgot to tell a couple of guns where to meet after the drive. I failed to tell the other guns not to pick up shot game in the cover behind them as that was to be the next drive. The beaters lost direction or the pheasants ran out as there wasn't a stop. I now accept that for everybody else to relax on a shooting day I have to stay alert. When I shoot elsewhere with friends then I can happily relax. I am sure this is the same for all who run shoots.

Friends who come from afar and stay the night prior to a shoot are sometimes not immune to the dramas. Tom Cook from Sennowe, a large estate with a good shoot in Norfolk, volunteered to come out on night patrol later after dinner. We tip-toed round in the dark as I pointed out two pheasants in a thorn bush to the left or steered him away from where partridges were jugging on a strip of plough. Suddenly there was a crashing of undergrowth as we walked along a narrow path through the End wood. Tom's stick went up as he thought we were being attacked by poachers. I calmed him down and dispatched a fox we must have driven ahead of us into the snare I'd set that evening. Shaking a little, Tom said he wondered if his keepers spend their nights out in the woods? Certainly his guests are not disturbed from their port after dinner to patrol the hallowed coverts of Sennowe!

The sad fact is that though still economical the costs of running the shoot have escalated. In 1993 when the first edition of *Will's Shoot* was published the costs worked out at about £1000 a year, which represented only £1 per head of game shot or £2 per head of reared game.

Since then a number of factors have brought me nearer the real world of shoot costs. There were no keepering expenses when I did it all myself. The price of game was £4 per brace of pheasants which made a significant contribution to beaters' costs which were half what they are now. Beaters' pay now is still in no way the reason anyone goes beating. They come because they love the day and the cash is no more than expenses and a drink or two at the end of the day. When I did the keepering the guns made a collection for the beaters and helpers which again contributed. Now Brian is a fully fledged keeper and so rightly I ask guns to thank him direct. There were no game crop costs in the early days but now though patches are modest by most shoot standards, there is a cost. So my expenses have risen and receipts have

Beaters gather at the end of a drive.

become virtually non-existent. Nevertheless I love the whole year of the shoot and the opportunity to invite a few mates on shoot days is a small way to reciprocate sport I have enjoyed with them. This pleasure to me is incalculable and so my costs are acceptable. I am actually very fortunate that the scale being small keeps the whole project affordable and so no commercial let days or syndicate members are necessary to subsidise it. I do not propose to look any further into the costs as I may not like what I see. I do know that when I look at the overall income produced from the fisheries, tree business and rentals that the base of the financial pyramid well supports the top of it which is the shoot and wildlife sanctuary. They earn nothing but give me and others a greater wealth of joy than any dividend or director's remuneration should it be a quoted company on the stock exchange.

We have five days shooting before Christmas, with eight guns and a dozen beaters with as many dogs. The most senior helpers, those over eighty, are promoted as 'stops'. In a briefing, I explain that we have the limit on duck and that foxes are not

The game cart.

to be shot. There are four or five drives in the morning with everyone on foot walking from drive to drive. This is hardly strenuous as during the morning we shoot over only about thirty-five acres (approx.16 hectares) . It may seem that eight guns is rather a lot for such a small shoot but the layout of the woodland is such that each gun has cover behind him to which pheasants can fly. No-one gets a disproportionate amount of the shooting and the bag is made up from each gun perhaps having a chance of a few birds each drive. The guns are stood to make the pheasants most sporting, often in a small glade or amongst tall willows where snap shots test the reaction of even the most accomplished.

Friends, some of whom come from grand acres, large farms or smart syndicate shoots, all enjoy the spirit of this mini shoot, confined between areas of urbanisation. There is banter between the guns who joke about the bird that landed by the Belisha beacon or the 'stop' by the traffic lights. Shirley Deterding always refers to the last drive over the horseshoe lake as 'The Council House drive' as all the guns can see are rooftops above the tall hedge line over which the pheasants are driven.

A number of keepers have been amused to accompany their 'Gov'nors'. However it is no place for standing on ceremony, there are no great flushes of birds requiring loaders and so Tom, the head keeper from Six Mile Bottom, who came one day with Noel Cunningham Reed, soon found himself co-opted as a 'stop' for the first drive. Afterwards he was all smiles, as it had been such a good position from which to see the drive and he'd watched his boss, a connoisseur of guns and ballistics, account for nine fine cock pheasants with as many shots of his home loaded .410 cartridges.

We all then end up at the old wooden shed in the yard where beater friends and guns gather for sustenance, a chance to chat and joke about the morning and swap stories of other days shooting. At this stage the beaters get their noses into their 'dockey' bags having worked up an appetite. Soup, sherry and biscuits are welcome cheer for the guns who lunch later at the local pub.

On one bitterly cold day, when we gathered in a rusty old Nissen hut in the yard where the tortoise stove had been stoked up all morning by Ken to warm us, we found that not only was it virtually red hot but so too was the chimney, a cast iron pipe which projected through the roof. It had set light to the generations of old starlings' nests between the corrugated tin roof and the lining.

All the guns and beaters formed a chain, passing buckets of water from the nearest pond to Ken perched on top of a ladder, dousing the flames to quell the fire. By the time it was extinguished we were all warmed up and stood at the far end of the shed away from the heat of the stove!

After the break we set forth to do the two lake drives. This involves blanking out one large holding area of woodland from which the pheasants can run either left up a hedgerow to the Horseshoe drive or right handed into the cover behind the Lodge Lake. The beating line then reforms to continue driving this strip of woodland away from home. The birds flush at various stages and curl sideways out across the Lodge Lake over the guns on the far bank or fly back over the guns either side of the strip.

Usually at this stage the duck are flying well from lake to lake making for a variety of shots, and the guns can expect pheasants or mallard from any angle in front or behind.

Pickers-up Terry and Robin Wise, a top trial handler and trainer of working dogs, are both kept busy after the drive with retrieves in water or from the thick surrounding cover. Robin is the wife of Dr Doug Wise, probably the country's leading game and poultry expert. He taught at the University Veterinary School in

The final drive over the Horseshoe Lake makes an attractive setting for the guns.

Robin and Terry have rarely missed a day's picking-up at Hauxton over the thirty seasons.

Cambridge before he retired. In those days he also ran the game farm which produced the pheasant poults for the shoot. Robin is a great help on shooting days and not only is so good with her dogs but such great company. On occasions guns have been known to have lost a fictitious bird and 'chat up' Rob while her dogs hunt in vain!

The dense cover is ideal for spaniels, in fact with beaters alone very few birds would be flushed. Whether great characters have spaniels or spaniels make great characters, either way they seem to go together. Bob, the rat man, the local pest officer, is no exception. It is debatable as to whether he's as tall as he is round or square as he is short, certainly his smile is always broad. He is as strong as an ox and will crash through the thickest of undergrowth with spaniels all around him. Terry is a retired local policeman, who enjoys his dogs and is seen picking up on the best shoots in the area. However, before promotion to picker-up at Hauxton he was always in the thick of the cover with a well-controlled spaniel. He also brought a Jack Russell terrier which he carried under his arm between drives and then put nose to cover at the beginning of a drive, introducing it like a ferret to a rabbit burrow. There was no game left in that wood by the time the drive was over, when he'd again be carried under Terry's arm to the next.

The element of surprise is exciting on a shooting day and occasionally geese fly over in range and provide a shot. Sandy Reed shot one, when as a back gun at a drive, and returned to join the rest of the party dragging this great gander behind him. Colin Willock, wrote as 'Town Gun' for *Shooting Times* for so many years prior to his death in 2005, was always quick with a literary reference; he suggested Sandy carry it for the rest of the day like the Ancient Mariner's albatross. Sandy exclaimed that he'd done penance enough carrying it as far as the game cart!

On another occasion, after a long journey, Colin arrived late and missed the briefing and careful instructions about the limit of four duck or six shots. So when the duck started to fly he, being a great wildfowler, shot four duck in quick succession and then another one or two while Prue Coats standing with him tried to draw his attention to the rules. Colin, being hard of hearing and whose head was cocooned in earmuffs, just interpreted her excitement as enthusiasm for his performance and yet another couple splashed down from a great height before the message ever got through! He told the story against himself so well in the next 'Town Gun' article.

After shooting, the game is laid out and counted. I am not suggesting a great ceremony as is customary on the continent but I do like to see game carefully braced up and displayed or hung in the game larder as a mark of respect for the quarry which has provided the day's sport. It is a good opportunity for guns, beaters and all involved to chat over the memorable moments of the day. We are all involved in the sport together and I like to see everybody enjoy the day as a mutually friendly party.

The guns, wives and friends then set off in convoy across country to our home for a late lunch; one will be asked to be barman until I arrive later, having thanked and settled up with the beaters in cash or game.

In early years it was not only the influence of Archie Coats as the amateur keeper of his amazing little shoot at Towerhill, that helped me with the shoot, but his wife,

The game is laid out at the end of the day when all guns and helpers can gather for a chat.

Prue's, influence was considerable on the lunch. Those who were privileged to experience her gastronomic feasts will know that they were unique and competition or comparison unthinkable. However, the formula of having a large lunch to compensate for a small shoot was the original encouragement to try putting on a day at Hauxton at all.

My wife, Gina, is not madly enthusiastic about the shooting but is a brilliant cook. Her father was a director of some of London's top hotels, a specialist in high quality catering and amongst a multitude of achievements, organised over one hundred Buckingham Palace Garden tea parties over twenty-five years. It was not surprising therefore that Gina soon developed a talent for fine shoot lunches at home.

With a four mile journey from the shoot it means that it is not feasible to do other than eat afterwards. I feel this has a number of advantages, the most important of which is that the pheasants have time to settle down, feed and go up to roost in peace. This is particularly important on a small shoot. Also, the beaters can finish earlier and have no waiting about for guns to reappear after a normal midday lunch which invariably takes longer than anticipated. On larger shoots this is not so much a problem as the time can be constructively used blanking in, prior to the first drive after lunch. A final advantage of the late lunch is that guns can fully relax, the meal is not hurried and so due justice can be done to the food and full appreciation of the efforts of the cook.

Depending on numbers we either sit down cosily at the long kitchen table or, if there are too many in the party, we serve the courses, buffet style, in the kitchen and then people find a seat somewhere in the sitting room. However, the menu is then limited to something easily eaten with only a fork as while the ladies are so elegant and clever at juggling plates, cutlery and glasses, we chaps are really more comfortable with less of a balancing act and everything firmly on a table. Therefore we've tended to favour sitting down in the kitchen even if it is more cramped.

For the past ten years that successful formula has had to change. The problem came when my son, Henry, was introduced to shooting. I wanted to put on an extra day just before Christmas when the boys were back from school. This was a father and son day on which I would arrange the draw so the fathers drew even numbers and boys uneven; this spaced boys and dads alternately. Nothing gives us dads more fun than enjoying our children participate in sports for which we have a passion. Our son's first pheasant is more exciting than any we shoot ourselves. So all a great success, having increased the number reared to allow an extra day, the next generation were enthusiastically launched.

However, the snag was at home where with Christmas looming all energies on the domestic front were focused on seasonal festivities with all the work entailed. It was the straw that broke the camel's back for shoot lunches at home which had originally been four and the helpers' day big evening meal, but had increased to six or seven.

Gina is a perfectionist in the kitchen and understandably did not want to spend the shooting season cooking. So we now eat at a local pub on most days except the helpers' big do in early January. The pub lunches are fine but I miss the opportunity to offer home hospitality though it was not me who had most of the work for that. Mind you I am pleased not to spend all night washing up afterwards.

The Helpers' Day

After the five main days before Christmas I organise the helpers' day in early January. On most shoots the beaters' day is right at the end of season but at Hauxton all those who assist are close friends who help in so many ways throughout the year with other activities. For years Reg has been a fantastic help with tree work, road maintenance, hedge cutting or whatever. His brother, Philip, provides a ton or two of corn surplus after seed trials. John Barnard has been there at the 'drop of a hat' if there is any work or problem with the fisheries. Peter Elliott, an old friend who has built up a very successful fruit farming enterprise over the road, has helped for years with trees, security, machinery or whatever. Young James, son of Bob the rat man, would take over feeding when the rest of us went up to Scotland to walk up grouse

The line-up of Hauxton shoot helpers has changed little over the years except for our ages and three key people who have sadly died.

in Invernesshire. This was on hilly, new forestry ground, ploughed into enormous ridges and furrows which was previously good heather moor and then became 'kill or cure' walking, producing for many helpers their first grouse but for others of us, hopefully not our last! Sadly the forest is now twenty feet (9m) tall and abandoned long ago by grouse.

This helpers' day team of some dozen or so friends all have been actively involved for quite a number of years. As they seldom have the opportunity of much shooting I like to have their day when there is still sufficient game about for everyone to hopefully get some sport.

It has become known as 'the big day'. This relates more to the number of guns than the size of the bag but is the most special day of the season for everyone involved. There are normally fourteen guns, Carl and Roger when they were alive were unable

1	John Barnard (works for the Environment Agency) – always helped with fisheries and shoot.
2	Jen Bradford, wife of Bob, mother of James – chief 'Stop' and bakes tasty mince pies for all on December shoot days.
3	Andy works with Bob on the council.
4	Brian Morley – now head keeper, fishery bailiff and my right hand man on all activities at H. Good at all the wide variety of jobs about the place and a most observant and natural countryman.
5	Bob 'the rat man' Bradford, a great character and friend – so good with spaniels and humour! A real countryman.
6	Spencer Morley, Brian's nephew, worked with us on the tree business part-time while qualifying. Now tree officer for a London Borough – except on shoot days.
7	Reg Watson – friend and great help on trees and all hedge cutting. I'm godfather to his son, Henry.
8	WG, the author and under-keeper when allowed near Brian's pheasants!
9	Philip Watson – brother of Reg, kindly produces free corn surplus from seed trials.
10	Peter Elliott, a great helper on trees and friend for many years – as a boy I was sent to his mother, a school teacher, to try and teach me to read!
11	Bernie Sewell, poacher turned game-keeper. Always willing to help in any way, especially skilled with a chain saw.
12	John Rider, a new member of the team – keeps all amused with sarcasm and unrepeatable stories.
13	Chris Hughes, son of Roy the senior tree pruner, has taken up both fishing and shooting since coming to help on the shoot.
14	James Bradford (son of Bob), a chip off the old block – mustard-keen on shooting, very good shot and great cricketer.
15	Lindsay Cunningham (ex policeman) – joker in the pack, with great sense of humour. A friend who voluntarily helped keepering for a number of years, now a member of the tree team.
16	Brian Jewitt – well known in the Field Trialling world and loves the variety of retrieves possible at Hauxton and trout fishing in the summer.
17	Robin Wise – good friend and a v. skilled doggy lady with dogs that can both work picking up and win trials. As her dogs contribute to the bag so too does her charm and personality add to the day.
18	Terry Edwards (ex policeman). Picker up at Six Mile Bottom if not at H, there's a man with a sense of priorities! Good with spaniels and labs and in the past brought his Jack Russell beating.

to beat so they stood at each drive, the others are split into two teams who beat and stand alternately. For safety reasons the beating team are not armed and this also prevents any confusion or accusation as to whether a bird flushed was going forward over the standing guns or back over the beaters! I try to see that there is an even chance of shooting and so we do eight drives, pairing the better potential drives and the lesser ones. One problem is, of course, that there are only half the beaters, dogs or stops for each drive compared with a normal day and some pheasants 'tuck in' or 'run out' and so avoid the guns. However, there are usually birds in every drive and the standard of the shooting is very accurate especially considering how few opportunities many of them have pheasant shooting in a season.

After these manoeuvres some guns go to the Everglades to flight pigeons whilst the remainder drain the last coffee from their flasks, before manning the hides around the Lodge Lake to flight the duck. Later still just as the flight is ending there is sometimes the sound of sporadic, distant honking and a minute later Canada geese circle and drop in to offer the last shots of the day.

Geese often produce the highlight shot of someone's day. However, I used to ask guns not to shoot the greylags as numbers were not yet sufficient. One day as a mallard flew upwind high over Bob he upped his gun and with a mighty swing

Bob and John tie up the game between drives.

killed it cleanly. However, simultaneously a greylag passed over, going downwind in the opposite direction, from behind, and apparently flew into the shot. Those who witnessed the event, of course, made much of the demise of the forbidden goose which Bob swore he never ever saw but he was christened 'Greylag Bob' nevertheless!

My son, Henry, felt he was not eligible to shoot unless he had helped beating with the team on the preceding shoot day which was at the beginning of his school holidays. When he shot his first ever pheasant he got two in the same drive, both good crossers high over the trees on the corner of the Everglades. I don't know who was the more thrilled, him or me standing with him, a very proud father. The day's other highlight was when Terry, the policeman, let out a surprised cheer as he shot two mallard, his first ever right and left. He has never claimed to be a great shot but to wait until his mid fifties to achieve this does show considerable patience! Well done Terry!

At the end of the helpers' day a typical bag could be thirty-five pheasants, eighteen mallard, two tufted duck, three moorhen, two rabbits (caught by dogs), twenty-four pigeons, two woodcock, three Canada geese, one snipe, one magpie and one squirrel (probably after four shots). So a total of perhaps ninety-two head after a very sporting day.

This is followed by an enormous meal at home when, with three tables set at angles like dominoes right across the kitchen, we can sit up to eighteen, packed in tight shoulder to shoulder. Reg will carve two loaves of bread into one inch steps while I serve Gina's legendary cottage pie, steaming from the oven with a brown, crispy top. A big square dish serves six proper portions. It's no good serving Brian or Reg with Nouvelle Cuisine samples for slimming nuns or 'boil in the bag' portions of fish only suited for invalids.

These are hungry lads after a long day. A chockie pud of some sort is always popular to follow after which, with the port and cheese, Bob announces the result of the day's sweepstake. Then I take the opportunity to say a few words to thank all for their help throughout the season. The day is a climax of the year's teamwork and I cannot help being rather repetitive each year on this occasion, pointing out how it could not work without the support, help and good will of all present.

The most senior will usually respond on their behalf with a few kind words of how they have all enjoyed the day and everything at Hauxton, whether work or sport during the year.

Bob very kindly presents Gina with an enormous plant or colossal box of fruit for which they have all contributed – a very touching gesture and much appreciated.

What a wonderful thing it is to enjoy a day's sport with friends.

Later in January there are three more shoots. A day for chums run as a full day, then two further forays with about half a dozen key helpers all shooting. Two may stand as forward guns while the others drive the cover with dogs. These days are always a lot of fun and successful as we drive many of the woods in the reverse direction to normal, which tends to catch out cocks which have learned to avoid the guns.

By then we are really trying and start early to fit in up to fifteen drives before flighting the pigeon, duck and then geese. These days can produce the most mixed bags of the season.

7 · PARTING SHOT

The Laurent Perrier Award (now the Purdey Award) was a special milestone not only for the honour of winning, but for the opportunity to write about the work put into the place and take stock of the achievements. The encouragement through the years as each step was taken, each tree or shrub planted or water area created, was a stimulus for the next stage. The first twenty years saw the completion of the main overall structure and since then the projects have been to further improve details, enlarging the area for orchids, improving feeding and nesting areas for duck, selective planting in the woods and implementing schemes to make new drives or improve existing ones.

Nothing ever stands still in nature and all habitat needs constant assessment and, if necessary, work to maintain or improve it. Woodland takes years to mature and is, at stages in its development, too dense, too dark, too open or too cold. Again variety is the important message and work in a block of woodland should be phased so that conditions are not all at the same stage. Some parts are thick and provide warm roosting, while other glades are coppiced, thinned or felled in rotation.

Over the years there have been a number of one day courses at Hauxton. As much of the success has depended on advice or literature from the Game Conservancy, it was gratifying, therefore, to be asked to run the first 'small' shoot management course in 1982. Hitherto their courses had centred on large farms or estates where successful shoots had been established for many years. It was an important step to encourage those who farmed on a smaller scale to show that it was possible to have a shoot and produce sport on a confined area. Also I felt this was politically good for the Game Conservancy to involve a much greater number of such enthusiasts as members rather than predominantly concentrating on the major landowners for support.

The course was titled 'Gardening for Game' which I felt summed up the cottage garden approach, where many varieties of plants are tended with great intensity on a small scale, as is the habitat and game at Hauxton. I would have liked that title to have been used for this book. However, the publisher pointed out the difficulty, suggesting it would then be planted in the 'Gardening' section in most bookshops!

In 1983 I was invited by the Game Conservancy to read a paper on the developments at Hauxton at the 'Wildlife on Man-Made Wetlands' symposium at Great Linford. This was later published together with the other, more highly technical and scientific, papers presented during the day.

Much of my magazine and book illustration work has reference drawn from Hauxton. These are included in the following books:

The Amateur Keeper, Archie Coats
Your Shoot, Ian McCall
The Fox and the Orchid, Robin Page
The Game Shot, Mike Barnes
The Woods Belong to Me, Angus Nudds
The Game Conservancy Council Report, 1983
The Hunting Gene, Robin Page

Also the place has attracted numerous articles and references in books. Some of these are by writer friends who have been involved and shot or fished there regularly. Robin Page, the well known author, lives in the nearby village of Barton.

The author describing features of the 'scrape' on a Game Conservancy course at Hauxton, April 1989.

A 'free thinker' and at times if not witty then controversial, often both! He's a marvellous writer and a very knowledgeable conservationist who fully appreciates the important contribution of country sports to the ecology of the countryside. His unbiased approach gives added strength to his opinions as he does not shoot, hunt or fish himself.

He has often visited Hauxton and used to come beating occasionally but after a few days decided the impenetrable cover was best left to spaniels and that his talent was more suited to tapping a typewriter than a stick. We've worked together on a number of successful books, in particular *The Fox and the Orchid* and *The Hunting Gene.*

Colin Willock has frequently shot at Hauxton and his marvellous little book called *Dudley, the Worst Dog in the World,* about his rough haired Jack Russell terrier, was the first book I ever illustrated.

John Humphreys has been a sporting friend for many years since we met over thirty years ago, appropriately at a pigeon lecture in Cambridge by Archie Coats. He has frequently shot and fished, both for trout and carp over the seasons. On one occasion we had an evening in September fishing for the end of season trout. Then at the sound of distant 'honking' from the Canada geese we threw down our rods, picked up our guns and hid up in the reeds, after a volley of shots we landed a brace of fifteen pounders!

I am grateful to John for contributing to the book with his Foreword. Few know the place better or enthuse as much about the management of small scale sporting Edens – on his seven acres (2.8 hectares) of manicured Hunters Fen, every blade of grass, rush, puddle and twig contribute to the wildlife, sport and atmosphere of the place. Who better to ask therefore to enrich this book with a few of his lyrical words. He was commissioned to write a double page article about the pits in the *Shooting Times* at the time of the Laurent Perrier Award. Those two pages summed up, better than I in the whole book, the spirit, aspirations, ambitions and atmosphere of the place.

The following magazines and books have referred to Hauxton.

The Great Shoots, Brian Martin
The Fox and the Orchid, Robin Page
The Shooting Times, Colin Willock, John Humphreys, Robin Page
The Sporting Gun, Mike Barnes
Insight, Mike Barnes
Horticultural Grower
The Field
The Greek Shooting Magazine
Country Sport
The Shooting Gazette

Country Life
Weekend Telegraph
The Times
Cambridge Evening News
Cambridge Weekly News
Countryman's Weekly
Insight
Dog World
BASC Shooting and Conservation
Game Conservancy Magazine
Sporting Gun Magazine
Farm and Country

Anglia Television
Radio Cambridge

Conclusion

Whilst the book is coming to a conclusion the project at Hauxton will I hope continue for many years. There is much still to do maintaining and improving the habitat for wildlife and game.

One of the reasons for the number of achievements over the years is that whilst I may have been rather dictatorial in my direction and ambition, there has been a positive pyramid of priorities. This is much more difficult if, as on many reserves, the management decisions are subject to a committee, which leads to a diluting of each policy culminating in compromise where nothing is actually developed to its full potential.

Basically my priority has been for the success of the shoot. This needs co-ordination with all the other interests. The overall diversity of habitat supports this and all the fauna and flora is absolutely in sympathy with the game interests.

The base of the pyramid is formed by the fisheries, specimen tree business and the yard. These all contribute to the total income but the importance of that does not conflict with the main interests of the shoot and wildlife. The fisheries, whilst producing a lot of sport for anglers in the summer, are not a problem during the shooting season. Both trout and carp are summer fish; with the trout fishery closed from 9 October, and with the carp being semi dormant in the winter, there are few anglers at that time. All anglers are strictly limited to their respective lakes and so there is no disturbance to wildlife or game elsewhere by the fishermen. The carp season does not open until 16 June, by which time duck, geese and warblers have usually all hatched and are unlikely to be disturbed.

The tree fields have game cover along the edges and the cultivation or work on the trees is rarely disturbing to game. The contractors who purchase the semi mature trees are not allowed to be on the site, lifting trees, on shoot days. Although they and their machinery may be busy on other days in the shooting season, they do not disturb the pheasants which are mainly in the woods.

The yard is an area of just over an acre (0.5 hectare) where the original gravel workings and office was based and this is let to a company which sells farm machinery. Their premises and workshop are fenced in and whilst of little value game wise, the rent contributes to supporting the whole venture and the chaps who work there are always so nice and help keep my old farm machines working.

Therefore everything contributes in harmony to the whole and even taking a wider view many of the seventy neighbours around the seventy acres help in one way or another, particularly with security.

The result of all this is that there are over four hundred species of plant on the site, 136 recorded species of bird with sixty-eight species breeding, over forty species of moss, over ninety species of fungi, twenty species of butterfly and an estimated two thousand man days sport each year. As a private reserve, there is the opportunity for people working on scientific or educational projects to monitor and experiment in an undisturbed habitat, which is sometimes not possible on public reserves.

With family and friends we have had a lot of fun and pleasure with children's

The original gravel yard is let to friends who for over twenty years have developed a successful business: The Cambridge Farm Machinery Company.

parties and barbecues, swimming and picnics, obviously at times and in places where nothing would be disturbed. When the children were young it was a great success with them to be taken through the woods by tractor and trailer for a 'jungle' party in a clearing with tent, camp fire, tug of war and lots of burnt sausage 'hot dogs'.

I am always gleaning ideas from people I meet or books I read which can possibly be of use for future improvements. There is so much to learn about all the wildlife and wonders of nature and the management of game for the sports we enjoy.

The Laurent Perrier Award is cherished not only as a tribute to the achievements of the past but as encouragement for the future. The champagne which accompanied the prize itself is enjoyed in the most appropriate way – as a small toast at the beginning of a shooting day when we raise our glasses to the 'future of sport and wildlife at Hauxton Pits'.

Cheers!

The most appropriate way of enjoying the prize for winning the Laurent Perrier Award is to have a taste at the beginning of a shooting day.

8 · TWELVE YEARS ON

As in nature nothing stands still in life. It is interesting therefore to look at how many aspects of Hauxton Pits have developed since *Will's Shoot* was first published in 1993. The all too obvious fact is that we are all that much older. However, it still seems only yesterday that thirty-five years ago, as a twenty-five year old art student, I raised my chewed pencil at the auction and found myself the proud but penniless owner of sixty-nine acres (28 hectares) of abandoned gravel pits. The truth is that in those early years of the shoot it was very much a 'boys'' shoot. Enthusiasm was high, energy was endless, expectations were modest and fun was enormous. Now as 'older boys' whilst most qualities are still as strong as ever, some energy has given way to nostalgia as we gather in the cabin for a midday break on one of our maraud days at the end of January. Friends who came to shoot in the early days were just told to crash into an area of woodland and find an opening where they could shoot. They now can tiptoe along a mown path to their peg.

Good Qualities That Have Not Changed

It is actually important firstly to acknowledge all the good things that have not changed. My ambitions are for ever being fine tuned but a sentence of my original introduction is as true as ever. 'My ambition has been to produce a diversity of habitat not just to attract rare species but where common ones are abundant; that on this tiny patch of England wildlife and game are not just a dream but a reality.'

Of the many acknowledgements of our project at Hauxton one of the most meaningful was a review by the eminent botanist, the late Dr Franklyn Perring. This was in the authoritative journal recording 'Nature in Cambridgeshire' and was written following a visit to the reserve shortly after publication of *Will's Shoot*. 'There may be some who still feel that shooting and conservation are incompatible: can I ask you to read this little book objectively and then think again. Would there be more wildlife at Hauxton today if the Trust had bought those gravel pits in 1970? I very much doubt it.'

Carl Smith, my fishery guru, and he never missed a shooting day.

These were the magnanimous words of the man who was underbidder at the auction on behalf of the then Cambridgeshire and Ely Naturalists Trust (now The Wildlife Trust of Cambridgeshire).

Whilst the area is the same except it was originally known as the 'seventy acre' shoot – I doubt the name 'Twenty eight point three two hectare' shoot would ever catch on.

The next very special fact is that of the fifteen friends who were helping then, twelve are still and most have done so since the first day's driven shooting in 1971. The other three, Roger, Carl and Mark are, I am sure, still with us each day in spirit. The few new members of the team are of the younger generation, relatives of the originals.

The loss of our three senior friends at the end of the millennia was both sad and salutary. None of us are getting younger but it gives me great pleasure to welcome those who can no longer take an active role with the beaters and there are always important jobs. So long as they want to be with us we will enjoy their company. Mark Bradford was still coming to shoots until he was ninety. Originally with his lab picking up, then when the dog died of old age I suggested Mark's little white farm pick-up would make a good game cart if he would kindly bring it and be in charge of game. He would give Carl, a mere octogenarian, a ride from drive to drive and then both would act as stops. While the heart was willing the body was there until the end. The local paper published a good photograph of Mark trout fishing at Hauxton on his ninetieth birthday. It was a wild, wet and windy day but in full waterproof weather gear Mark was casting determinedly into the gale with the enthusiasm of a boy on his first outing.

Roger was not so lucky and died in his sixties. He had always been a heavy smoker and this, combined with working in the sawdust of his workshop, eventually took toll of his lungs and heart. In his latter years he had developed his skill from a carver of wooden decoys to that of a great art form creating possibly the finest carved waders and wildfowl of anyone in the world. He won virtually every class of any competition he entered until the only way up was to become the senior judge of such exhibitions. He had taken a craft into an art form but sadly few art galleries acknowledged this at the time. I am very proud of my special collection of his work, our sitting room mantelpiece has no Wedgwood or Royal Doulton china but the gracious curves of a Redshank, Black tailed Godwit and Greenshank and on the glass topped coffee table a cock teal forever swims. All bring memories of the man and his skills.

Roger introduced himself to me a day or two after the auction when I acquired the pits. He had been the voluntary warden for the site and we immediately recognised our common goals and interests. A very sensitive chap with a dislike of change; however he came with me through all the development of woodland and water. It was the water habitats for wildfowl and fish that were his real love. He looked after the duck, feeding everyday and watching their flight every evening. He became the bailiff of the fisheries and saw no compromise or discretion with interpretation of the rules. 'No wading' in the trout fishery was interpreted very positively and one unsuspecting member standing on the edge with the toe of his wellington in the water was jumped on by Roger as if he'd been up to his armpits in body waders. The rules were adhered to!

Roger was always good with his dogs and picked-up on every shooting day and a succession of them now lie in the dog cemetery on 'The mound', a sacred corner where we all bury our Hauxton canine friends. Rog helped with so many aspects of the work and was always willing to turn out for whatever the job was in hand. Such a loyal friend of the pits in every season, his heart was always in the place and, though sadly missed, I know his spirit will always be there.

I have written of my gratitude to Carl Smith in the fishery chapter, his loss too was enormous, but he left the foundation stones on which the fisheries have thrived. He was my fishing guru.

A story which still brings a smile is the occasion on a shoot day when he stood watching the guns on the Lodge Lake drive. They stand on the grassy bank and wait for a duck or pheasant to appear. Now a certain friend who in his youth was a practical joker – now an eminent Member of Parliament (is there a connection I ask myself?) – knew Carl was very serious about the water and fishery management. However, when Carl was watching he raised his gun and fired into the shallows at his feet. He then stepped forward and pulled out a trout and layed it on the bank. Carl approached me after the drive furious at the behaviour of my guest. What neither he, nor I knew until later was that the trout was already dead at the water's edge and Henry knew Carl would easily be wound up by his subsequent action of pretending to shoot it!

The Family

A family update is important as their formative years are now blossoming in their different interests. Jackie now in mid thirties went from an honours degree in construction management at Sheffield to an organic farming course at Broomfield Agricultural College. She saw that in the mid 90s there was not so much a production problem with many farmers going into growing organic food, but that there was a distribution and marketing opportunity. She opened her first shop in Heanor in Derbyshire and soon had customers coming from up to fifty miles away. She then had the opportunity to move her shop to an old well house on a farm in Kent that has been practising a special form of organic farming, biodynamic, for over fifty years. Perry Court Farm is in a SSSI valley near Canterbury and produces beef, vegetables and flour from its own stone grinding mill. Due later to lack of space she then moved into Canterbury taking space in the large SCATS (Southern Counties Agricultural Trading Society) store.

She then decided to come back to Cambridge to be near family and old friends and after looking at various potential shops we investigated the opportunity at Hauxton. The planners were very supportive of the conversion of our old shoot hut. The planning officer said they were keen on 'barn' conversions so we referred to it as a barn from then on. After a lot of work by Twink, Chris and Paul, my building friends, it had services, insulation, air-conditioning and new floor amongst a host of other details to turn our dilapidated shoot 'barn' into the Organic Health Emporium.

Two years on Jackie has developed a very successful, personalised business offering over three thousand lines of organic and special diet health food products sourced as locally as possible. She has won awards, given talks and been the subject of many articles and even featured complete with a big basket of fruit and veg on the cover of the East Anglian C.L.A. magazine. She is very settled and happy and I am thrilled to have her as a member of the family with her own business on the site. Not only can I see her everyday, but we can help each other running our various interests. She also sells our game with pride. It cannot be labelled 'organic' but it is certainly 'free range' and very local.

Penny is now thirty-something and happily married to Justin – a great chap and a very welcome addition to the family. He has learned to fish and shoot though, as he works in London, has little time for either at the moment. They produced our first

My daughter, Jackie, has developed a very successful business in the old shoot 'barn' – Organic Health.

grandchild on 29 January 2004. My helpers and I were having our final maraud that day and as I waited for pigeon late in the afternoon, I got the phone call with great news of the birth of our little Jemima. A good reason to break my rule of not carrying my mobile when out shooting. I remember clearly that as I was hearing this wonderful news, about the only pigeon which came did so, seeming to almost hover over my head before drifting off on the wind. It has to be very important news for me not to have dropped the phone and raised my gun to a pigeon. Jemima had her first walk around the lakes at Hauxton carried by her mother within a week and was watching her father and grandfather casting for a trout by six weeks old. How old does she need to be before she can help beating?

Henry, my son, has his heart also very much in the place though he lives away down at the tip of Cornwall where he paints and writes for London Galleries on

'A Reflective Moment', a painting by W.G.

Brian, my friend and right hand man, feeding the duck shallows.

British twentieth century art. This means trips home are now rare but he always enjoys participating in whatever is seasonal. One evening in May a year ago we had had one of our best evenings fishing on the Horseshoe Lake for trout. We sat on the bench as the sun set with trout still rising, musing on the special place it was – in fact how that acre of the lake and adjoining willows had produced so many great memories for him. He had learned to swim there one summer and skate one winter. He had shot rabbits on the grassy banks and his first duck and goose on that very spot he had caught trout that evening. He had shot some good pheasants driven over the lake as they climbed to clear the tall poplars and had his best pigeon flight in the willows on the corner. So a magic acre of England for him and equally for me that I should have created the stage on which such memories had been played out. That was the inspiration for a painting I worked on during the following week of the lake in May. I titled it 'A Reflective Moment' (see page 125).

Shoot Management

The details of improvements to feeding and watering systems for the poults in the release pens has been covered in the relevant chapter. However, there is an important development in the management which is that I have become ever more committed to weeks away painting or day to day activities that fill my happy life. I have had to learn to become a better delegator. As a very 'hands on' sort of chap this has been difficult. However, it has become much easier with the help of one person, Brian Morley. He and I have not only developed a very close friendship but a respect of each other's country ways. He has learned to do all the keepering, fishery and commercial tree work and is very much my right hand man. He is a good stockman with a sharp eye for day to day wellbeing of all in his charge. As he and I look round, whether together or independently, we always notice the same things that need attention: time to increase the wheat in the pellet mix in the release pens, moving hoppers, letting light into an area which may have become overgrown. A fox run worth a snare being moved or a block of trees needing pruning. Brian now manages it all while I am away and I have every confidence in him that in his totally 'unflappable' way all will be well. He is no less stubborn than ever but when the right day dawns the job will be done – lists are still an anathema to Brian – actually any paperwork but he has the memory of an elephant and a hide just as thick.

We have updated some of our machinery. A John Deere mini tractor is used for many jobs such as rotavating amongst the trees and lifting trees we move as standards using a back acting under-cutting blade. It is useful for cutting out paths on the shoot, feed rides and jobs all over the estate with the flail.

In addition to the original old grey Fergy and Fordson I later purchased a job lot of tractor and implements from the small farm at the other end of the village where Brian used to work. The owner sensibly decided it was more economical for his few fields to be contract farmed which meant both Brian and the machinery were redundant. I welcomed both man and machinery full time. This gave us a more powerful Massey Ferguson tractor which also has powered steering and a more comfortable seat – no wonder Brian recommended I purchased it when it became available. We also added a larger trailer, subsoiler and chisel plough deep cultivator as well as a powerful grass swipe which pulverises bramble and suckers on areas we want to keep clear.

A big investment in 1990 was the sinking of a borehole. We had suffered several drought summers and Hauxton pits without water is as dehydrating as for a man in a desert without water. For the fisheries, the waterfowl and aquatic habitat as well as for irrigating trees, water is essential. I had to bite the bullet and invest a total of thirty thousand pounds to produce a borehole which provides clear clean water from sixty-nine metres below in the greensand. This needed a three phase electricity supply and all the pumps, gauges and plumbing to set us up for the future. Luckily the trees had had a couple of good years of sales and fishery rents were stable but once again Mr Lloyds Bank helped with an increased overdraft.

The Shooting Day

Ever since winning the Laurent Perrier Award we have maintained the tradition of starting the day with a glass of their champagne. Such a sophisticated start may seem incongruous with the informal nature of the small scale shoot. However, it was a most appropriate way of drinking the prize but the cellar has had to be topped up from time to time since then to continue the celebration.

I never considered the Hauxton Pits Shoot to be worthy of a game card. However, the idea evolved and I had the ingredients for an original one and the skills as an artist to design it. The front was obvious – the cover of the book itself with the addition of appropriate 'Garfitti'. So on shoot days a set of cards are numbered and used for guns to draw their peg as well as having a crib sheet of the list of fellow musketeers.

As the old shoot hut is now Jackie's organic shop we used a mobile portacabin for a couple of seasons. In the summer of 2004 I built a sizeable extension to the original farm building. This has been rented by the Cambridge Farm Machinery Company for over twenty years. The friends who run it have been very successful in spite of the general agricultural depression and low profitability of farming in recent years. They have agencies for good machinery, which over the years has become larger and larger. The original workshop is now only big enough for servicing mowers, strimmers and chainsaws, but there was a serious need for a tall and large space under cover for work on the farm equipment. The end bay of this I have kept for my own tractors and implements which have been without a home for several years and would be best kept under cover. This section of the building will be our new home also for guns and beaters on shoot days for the midday break.

On a pinboard I display recent articles or information of interest to beaters and guns. There is also an ongoing list of friends who have shot at Hauxton with the year they first did so. Amazingly since 1971 that list extends to over two hundred and fifty and is always an interesting topic of conversation. 'Good heavens has he been here – didn't they make a set of table mats of all the presumptions and rude letters he wrote to hosts he'd been to shoot with?'

The format of the day is the same, we set off on foot for five drives on the wooded

Hauxton Pits – 1998 Winner
of
The Laurent Perrier Award

Featured in:

THE SHOOTING TIMES	COUNTRYMANS WEEKLY
THE SHOOTING GAZETTE	INSIGHT
THE FIELD	DOG WORLD
COUNTRY LIFE	BASC SHOOTING & CONSERVATION
COUNTRY SPORT	GAME CONSERVANCY MAGAZINE
WEEKEND TELEGRAPH	SPORTING GUN
DAILY TELEGRAPH	FARM & COUNTRY
THE TIMES	
CAMBRIDGE EVENING NEWS	
CAMBRIDGE WEEKLY NEWS	ANGLIA TELEVISION

WILL'S SHOOT
WILL GARFIT

Foreword by
John Humphreys

HAUXTON PITS

The Hauxton Pits shoot game card.

half comprising the Eastern thirty five-acres (14 hectares). However, the important change is that the trees are of course taller every year and so the quality of birds shown when flushed from game crops outside the woods is seasonally improving. They have to fly higher and higher over the little glades or windows in the woodland where the guns are placed. Equally on the final drive which is attractive as we fly the pheasants over the Horseshoe lake to the guns in a semi circle as they stand with their backs to the home wood. Behind the guns the poplars planted as setts into holes in the willows are now twenty years' old and about ninety feet (27 m) tall, way taller than the willow scrub surrounding them. These pheasants can be quite challenging on a good day.

With the advent of the lead shot ban for wildfowl a new policy was required at Hauxton. We could of course legally shoot pheasants and all but the duck with lead but what goes up must come down and so as at the end of winter the high water table sometimes means that over half the area of the shoot is under water. Therefore the duck could pick up shot even if it did not fall in the shallow margins of the lakes. For this reason I ask guns to use non-lead shot at all times. This is obviously more expensive but the modest number of cartridges used in a day at Hauxton will never bankrupt anyone.

For many years now the fact that constantly amazes me is that on such a small shoot the daily and seasonal bags are so consistent. The annual total head varies

Pheasants flushed from a game crop have to fly up the 'ramp' of smaller nursery trees to rise and fly high over the tall willows behind.

mainly by the number of rabbits and pigeon accounted for on other than organised shoot days. The intention for the latter is to produce a mixed bag in the region of one hundred head and this figure does remain surprisingly constant. Yes, we must be doing something right in overall management but even so I would expect birds to hold much better some years than others. I therefore feel the key principle of my original plan which was to spend time, energy and a certain amount of cash on improvement of the habitat was the foundation of success. It still is.

Habitat Yesterday and Today

There is no doubt that the work put in every year has paid great dividends. It is not obvious until one realises that the original tree cover was exclusively willow colonisation. This was mainly of three willow species. White willow (*Salix alba*), Goat willow (*Salix caprea*) and Grey willow (*Salix cinerea*). The latter two are commonly known as sallow or 'pussy willow' for they both have the furry silver catkins in early spring. There are other species and then the many hybrids. So the original landscape consisted of willows and water of the abandoned gravel workings left in a ridge and furrow formation across the site. Over time whilst maintaining some of this former habitat I have created the lakes from the wettest areas and mixed woodland on some of the dryer.

The life cycle of willows is short by comparison with other trees and it was a salutary example when one of the largest willows blew down in 2004. A tree was some thirty inches (75 cm) across and yet when I counted the rings in from the outer bark for thirty-four years to get back to 1970, the year I purchased the place, the tree then was a mere eight inches (20 cm) in diameter. However, this short life cycle enables us to act and improve the woodland diversity and the holes that appear can be planted with conifers for roosting on the dry banks or oaks in the damp areas. This has over the years produced a patchwork quilt of different species of varying sizes across each wood. Every year usually in February after the shooting season has ended we set about opening up a new glade here and there to keep the variety of species and age developing. This has created much better woodland for pheasants and small birds as well as looking attractive. The release pens need special care each spring to cut down some trees to allow more light to penetrate. In what we call the 'new' pen which was woodland planted in 1971 and became a release pen in 1981, those conifers are now past their sell by date for optimum roosting. Therefore each year we fell a small section and replant with Norway spruce to be the ideal roosting in ten to twenty years' time. It is a very short rotation therefore to keep the optimum condition. We prolong that time by topping the spruce at about fifteen to twenty feet (approx. 4.5 to 5 m) tall which keeps them with bushy tops for longer.

The Leylandii planted within willows have grown well in the partial shade. They have warmed up the edges of woods and are themselves favoured for roosting and for many birds for nesting. Ecologically the Leylandii is mainly misused in gardens as it produces such a large tree and causes great neighbourly disputes. However, if maintained as a hedge it makes an excellent tight shape and good background for other more decorative shrubs or plants in front.

The stage at Hauxton with its balance of open water, shallow scrapes, coppiced willow scrub, open glades, mixed aged woodland, open woodland created by the tree plantations, shelter belts and game crops all contribute to the picture, beautiful to look at and wonderful for all game and wildlife.

The glades are managed for orchids, shrubs are dotted strategically on woodland edges. For this I have increasingly favoured the wild privet *(Ligustrum vulgare)*. I used to plant species like laurel but regret introducing a species which has garden connotations and in any case the rabbits gnaw at the lower branches and so create a very draughty, bare area below. The wild privet is a natural and indigenous species. It grows fast and as rabbits do not like it, a thick bush with cover to the ground is good for blocking out the wind and creating flushing points for pheasants. It is easily managed at any stage of its growth. I planted a nursery strip of this right down the middle of our main game crop in the Mascal's drive. As the tractor has to turn at the ends it was easy to cultivate and plant the game crop each spring leaving the now central hedge. Each year we removed alternate bushes to plant out wherever needed. The central spine is permanent thick cover for pheasants and prevents flushing of too many birds at once from the maize either side.

The reed beds are managed around the lakes to create large enough territories for warblers to nest but also spaces between for the angler to fish – both are thereby managed for optimum mutual benefit without the other realising it. What an amazing surprise and joy it was on a November shooting day in 2004 to flush a bittern from one of these small areas of reed. It performed a leisurely fly past along the line of guns before doing the same in front of the beaters on the other side of the lake. It then floated like a moth to land in another reed bed. The first ever recording of a bittern was privilege enough but for it to be such a public sighting was a great bonus.

My Holistic View

Every bush and blade of grass has a purpose and on the small scale of Hauxton Pits it is a joy to manage it intensively. However, in recent years when on a summer evening, there may be a course run for the Game Conservancy, BASC, fishery management or even women's institutes or horticultural groups, I now find that after visiting sites to explain facts of management, game birds, release pens, wildfowl, trees or botany, we usually end up at the Horseshoe lake. The beauty is self evident but I ask the question 'are we doing all we do on our own patches of whatever scale to just get another few birds in the air or is there something more profound? Is there something deeper? Are there feelings we are not quite in touch with that fuel our belief and actions in the countryside?' For me and I suspect for others there is a fundamental wish to contribute to the future for those who come after as the many generations have done before us. We shooters and countrymen and women are perhaps privileged to be close to the hub of the natural wheel of life. We are in touch with our senses. Through our eyes the sights of beauty or drama in sunlight or storm. Through our ears the sounds of birds, the wind, the gurgling stream. The smells we notice sometimes subconsciously, some as sweet as the flowers, others as pungent as bubbles from a muddy pool. We have to touch a stone, run our hand over the bark of a beech. There is never a moment in nature that something is not there to be observed, heard, touched, smelled or in some way acknowledged and enjoyed.

Is it that deep down we know the truth, the fragile truth that life is dependent on light from the sun, the purity of water and the fertility of the soil? As we are dependent on those elements so are we each able individually to contribute to their well being. All of nature has the urge to procreate to carry genes forward but only mankind has the power and responsibility to do something about maintaining the environment – our life support system. There is a life force, a god, a universal energy

In two ways meaningful: to have the opportunity of creating the landscape and then twenty-five years later to paint it. 'The view from the end of the Lodge Lake.'

that is our guardian but mankind is often at conflict with those forces. We can all play our part by doing or helping change attitudes. Let that be fuelled by our own individual acknowledgement and celebration of the natural world about us and pass on that as well as our genes to our children and grandchildren.

As an artist I have spent much time alone in the landscape hoping that I may be in touch with my feelings and emotions and so express them in my paintings; more than that, I see evidence daily to support my holistic view and the bigger picture.

Botanical Interest

A natural progression from a quest to produce an ideal habitat for the benefit of game and wildlife is that of a developing interest in the overall flora on the site. The publication of the first edition of this book in 1993 included the appendix of 274 plants recorded. However, it was with a certain shame that I realised I did not actually know or recognise many of those listed by visiting botanists. This sparked off a new found great interest for me not only at Hauxton but wherever my travels or painting trips take me. I started by photographing every plant and flower through the seasons. I saw my little patch with new eyes and day by day had my old Yashika 35 mm camera with me. Photographer friends gave me a few pointers about botanical photography which included to always use a tripod, don't be afraid to experiment and for white and light coloured flowers either bracket exposures or reduce the aperture by one or two stops to prevent the subject being overexposed. This is due to the automatic exposure meter reading the neutral mid-tone of green foliage surrounding the flower. Although this produced beautifully recorded leaves the light coloured flowers were often seriously over exposed as they reflected so much light. Anyway my album collection rapidly grew. There were some pleasing photographs of which I was quite proud but others for the purpose of recording were either good photos of rather poor specimens or poor photographs of pristine ones.

My new found botanist friend, Philip Oswald, has been my guru and inspiration. The academia of Cambridge produces world class specialists in many fields. It was my very good fortune to find Philip who is a botanist of this class. He is a classicist and a man of great intellect who has been the professor in my quest for plants. I struggle madly to keep up intellectually with Latin or Greek names or botanical characteristics of a sub species of some plant of which those distinctive subtleties can only be seen through a 10x magnification lens – if it has not hybridised – in a good light – at a certain moment of its life cycle. However, Philip patiently acknowledges a trade-off that where intellect may struggle my enthusiasm more than compensates. Also that as an artist I have developed a certain skill in observation and so have found quite a number of new plants for the list by spotting something of which I may not know the name but do know I have not seen it before.

Over the next two years the collection of botanical photographs extended to two big albums and whilst most early photographs were taken using a 2x converter, a cheap and cheerful device which meant that I could photograph small flowers with the equivalent of a close-up lens. I later invested in a 'macro' lens which really enabled photographs to bring details of plants to life.

During the summer of my creeping around on hands and knees, Brian and Roger increasingly were amused. On one occasion I returned from a fortnight's painting trip and camera in hand went to inspect a patch of mouse-ear-hawkweed Philip had found on the area we call the 'Healthy bit'. The problem was that the rabbits had eaten every flower of the plants. I had therefore put a wire cage over them to see if, when protected, a flower head could emerge for me to photograph. As I approached the spot there amazingly in the cage were not only the yellow daisy like flowers of the species of hawkweed but a larger more exotic botanical specimen altogether. With caution I lifted off the wire and there was this exquisite large conical flower with petals as white as porcelain. I had never seen anything like it outside a tropical greenhouse. At that moment a gust of wind came and this jewel collapsed, blown over. Yes, I had been truly set up – it was a plastic lily Roger and Brian had found in the churchyard! I photographed it and it is in my album as *'Hauxtonia pretensis'* – maybe even more appropriate would have been *'pratensis'*. However, you will not find it on Philip Oswald's authorised and updated list in the new appendix of flora.

The new list now includes 408 plants identified on the site, a considerable addition of 134. The majority of these were probably on the site before but not recorded. Some others have been introduced. Certainly several new chalk downland species were included in the selected wildflower mix when I created a bank of chalk marl excavated from the old stock pond when it was enlarged and deepened. This opportunity added another potential habitat for a specific flora. Species in the mix which have been particularly successful and now dominate are Birdsfoot trefoil, Wild Basil and Marjoram. Vipers Bugloss has successfully colonised the bank of the pond itself. It is important when introducing new plants to ensure they are from authentic British stock. Too many commercial 'wild flower mixes' include foreign clones.

Philip has been such a help and inspiration and I am excited to follow in his footsteps as he stalks like a heron with long legs and purposeful steps, his head inclined as his eyes scan the vegetation ahead for a prize on which to pounce. An unsuspecting diminutive plant will become the subject of a learned discourse on the origin of its name from an obscure Greek myth or how he had found a sub species of the same plant on Mount Athos twenty years earlier.

As a true botanist all plants are known by their scientific Latin name. In respect of this as an acknowledgement to Philip Oswald I felt it important now to include the Latin as well as the English name for plants on the list in the appendix. His knowledge is prodigious and yet his enquiring mind often leads any query to be forwarded to fellow world authorities who specialise in the appropriate field of investigation. I also am welcomed as a guest on courses he leads elsewhere in the county with the U3A group (University of the Third Age). Certainly they are welcome at Hauxton as often as Philip likes to bring them.

Neighbours, Public, Children and Visitors

I would like to think that I am aware of the ever changing public perception of the countryside, its management, its sports and wildlife. I have about as many neighbours whose gardens back on to the shoot as I have acres. Over the years I have

The southern marsh orchid: an exciting new species of which a group appeared on the bank of the Horseshoe Lake in 2004.

met many and got to know some well. I am pleased to say that there is none that I would feel uncomfortable about knocking on their door. However, on occasion I have had reason to call to discuss something about which I am unhappy. It may be children trespassing, dogs causing disturbance to game or the owner dumping garden rubbish and attracting rats. However, I am quite clear that the wrong time to act is while I am annoyed or worse angry. This would lead to a confrontation which is not constructive. If one is confronted by an angry person there are two ways of reacting. One is confrontation, the other submission, both can result in resentment and not willing co-operation. I therefore wait until I am calm and controlled and can discuss the situation in a way as to enrol the person with my vision, explain how their dog does harm disturbing game and wildlife on this special area much of which they enjoy seeing in their gardens or on their bird table. I am more comfortable as a diplomat than dictator. I like to encourage people to choose to follow with sound reason than provoke and threat to produce a required action. This works for me and I have no neighbours of whom I know to have other than a friendly relationship.

I have become more proactive in welcoming not only parties on the game, wildlife or fisheries management but groups as diverse as village horticultural societies, women's institutes, history societies, young farmers, art groups, school parties and once a year Jackie's shop Organic Health customers. I used to worry about attitudes to the shooting on such a place of beauty but by explaining clearly the purpose and management of all aspects affecting game and wildlife, I have yet to have anything but interest and appreciation for what is going on.

I do believe that we who are passionate about the country and our sports are too hidden behind our activities. By coming out and welcoming groups of people from whatever angle we have the opportunity of dispelling the fear of the unknown. The big high walls, many built by Napoleonic wartime prisoners around great estate parks are wonderful but can understandably lead those on the outside to have misconceptions about things on the inside. If we do not know or understand we naturally have a fear of it. Fear is a negative emotion and can lead to misplaced actions. So I feel it is important to share the vision, enrol the hearts and stimulate support. I usually have the visits in the summer when the lakes are beautiful, the birds singing and flowers of the season bejewelling the scene. It is then easy to extol the benefits of wardening, keepering and game management.

I am fortunate to have no rights of way over the ground and the success is only possible on an area without public disturbance except by the controlled way of welcomed groups and parties. I fear the CROW act will have a serious impact on wildlife if public access is extended to include further fragile habitats in the country. On the other hand the national parks and wildlife reserves are managed well for the balance of people and wildlife.

Education

I would like to see more opportunities for children to visit the reserve. The Countryside Foundation is a successful and active organisation promoting a better understanding by children of the working countryside. We tried to see if a major scheme could be organised for the children of Cambridgeshire. One afternoon in the summer an exploratory visit of representatives from schools in the county was organised by the Countryside Foundation. The support was very encouraging and fifteen of the seventeen schools approached were represented by enthusiastic teachers. I led the visit around the reserve and we ended with a brainstorming session as to how to make it happen. Then the depressing truth appeared. In spite of this really enthusiastic group of teachers with a will to achieve this there are so many bureaucratic restrictions. It would all have to be part of a planned school curriculum. Funds for transport were likely to be restrictive, the Health and Safety procedures would be daunting. A classroom or visitor centre would be needed for wet weather with loos for boys, girls, ladies, gents and the disabled. In spite of such teacher willingness the scheme was doomed.

However, I have seen another route to children's involvement and that is not through schools but through parents. I have had some successful visits when in groups parents bring their children and then relate family experiences to the new ones seen on a walk. No restrictions of red tape – no problem with weather – supervision – and it was fun because we could make it so. The children and parents loved it and everyone benefited with no costs, classrooms or bureaucracy. Children are our future and the future of our landscape and wildlife.

This has led me on to a bigger picture from which Hauxton has been my springboard. It is early days but from an idea initiated by the Woodland Trust for a new large wood in Cambridgeshire, I found myself leader of the working party to make this a reality. This in turn led on to identifying an area in the south west of the county where, scattered along the boulder clay ridge, are the last vestiges of ancient forest. My vision expanded to link these with woodland as suitable habitats which, together with other new woodland and landscape initiation, could create a much larger ecological scheme within a primarily arable area. With the unanimous support of all landowners approached this has become a real possibility and a co-ordinated plan is being prepared by professional consultants specialising in this field. The Woodland Trust, County Wildlife Trust and others are all enthusiastic to bring their own expertise to this scheme. This is an opportunity on a big scale to create a very special asset in the county for wildlife ecology and the future landscape.

Does not life move in a mysterious way? How could that young boy who first was taken bird watching in the gravel pits by his father know that it was to become such an important element of his life. A life that has enabled so many to enjoy sporting, environmental or educational experiences there. For me the opportunities of introducing my children to sights, sounds and the sports I hold dear and furthermore the subjects for a number of my most heart filled paintings. Above all, it has provided so much pleasure and joy through the years, the seasons, the days and each hour spent there.

May you too see something in the story of your life that creates optimism for the future from your pleasures of the past by actions of the present, so that the world around us is full of the sunshine of life.

Appendix 1

Birds Recorded
at Hauxton Pits
1969-2004

Great crested grebe*
Little grebe*
Cormorant
Shag
Heron
Purple heron
Bittern
Mallard*
Teal*
Mandarin duck
Garganey
Gadwall
Widgeon
Pintail
Shoveler
Tufted duck*
Pochard
Goldeneye
Ruddy duck
Goosander
Greylag goose*
White-fronted goose
Pink-footed goose
Snow goose
Barnacle goose
Canada goose*
Mute swan*

Bewick's swan
Buzzard
Sparrow hawk*
Osprey
Hobby
Merlin
Peregrine
Kestrel*
Red-legged partridge*
Grey partridge*
Pheasant*
Water rail*
Moorhen*
Coot*
Lapwing*
Little ringed plover*
Golden plover
Snipe*
Jack snipe
Woodcock*
Curlew
Bar-tailed godwit
Green sandpiper
Wood sandpiper
Common sandpiper
Marsh sandpiper
Redshank

Greenshank
Greater black-backed
  gull
Lesser black-backed
  gull
Herring gull
Common gull
Black-headed gull
Common tern
Arctic tern
Stock dove*
Woodpigeon*
Collared dove*
Turtle dove*
Cuckoo*
Barn owl
Little owl
Tawny owl*
Swift
Kingfisher
Green woodpecker*
Greater spotted
  woodpecker*
Lesser spotted
  woodpecker*
Skylark*
Swallow*

House martin
Sand martin*
Carrion crow*
Rook
Jackdaw
Magpie*
Jay*
Great tit*
Blue tit*
Coal tit*
Marsh tit
Willow tit
Long-tailed tit*
Treecreeper*
Wren*
Mistle thrush*
Fieldfare
Song thrush*
Tree sparrow
Redwing

Blackbird*
Wheatear
Whinchat
Nightingale*
Robin*
Cetti's warbler
Grasshopper warbler*
Reed warbler*
Marsh warbler
Sedge warbler*
Blackcap*
Whitethroat*
Lesser whitethroat*
Willow warbler*
Chiffchaff*
Goldcrest*
Firecrest
Spotted flycatcher*
Pied flycatcher
Dunnock*

Meadow pipit*
Pied wagtail*
Grey wagtail
Yellow wagtail
Great grey shrike
Red-backed shrike
Starling*
Greenfinch*
Goldfinch*
Siskin
Linnet*
Redpoll
Bullfinch*
Chaffinch*
Brambling
Yellowhammer*
Corn bunting
Reed bunting*
House sparrow*
Tree sparrow

Butterflies Recorded at Hauxton Pits

Large skipper	Small tortoiseshell	Meadow brown
Small skipper	Peacock	Gatekeeper
Large white	Red admiral	Ringlet
Small white	Comma	Wall
Green-veined white	Common blue	Speckled wood
Orange-tip	Small copper	Holly blue
Brimstone	Small heath	Clouded Yellow

Appendix 3

FLORA RECORDED
AT HAUXTON PITS

My great thanks to Philip Oswald for his inspiration and help to discover and record the 408 species listed. Nomenclature, both Latin and English follows *Field Flora for the British Isles* and *New Flora of the British Isles* 2nd edn by Clive Stace (Cambridge University Press 1999 and 1997.)

Agrimony • *Agrimonia eupatoria*
Alder, Italian • *Alnus cordata*
Alkanet, Green • *Pentaglottis sempervirens*
Amaranth, Common • *Amaranthus retroflexus*
Apple • *Malus domestica*
Archangel, Yellow (silver-blotched) • *Lamiastrum galeobdolon subsp. argentatum*
Ash • *Fraxinus excelsior*
Aspen • *Populus tremula*
Avens, Wood • *Geum urbanum*

Barley, Wall   *Hordeum murinum*
Bartsia, Red   *Odontites vernus*
Basil, Wild   *Clinopodium vulgare*
Bedstraw, Lady's   *Galium verum*
Beech • *Fagus sylvatica*
Bellflower, Clustered • *Campanula glomerata*
Bellflower, Trailing • *Campanula poscharskyana*
Bent, Black • *Agrostis gigantea*
Bent, Common • *Agrostis capillaris*
Bindweed, Field • *Convolvulus arvensis*

Bindweed, Hedge • *Calystegia sepium*
Bindweed, Large • *Calystegia silvatica*
Birch, Silver • *Betula pendula*
Bird's-foot-trefoil, Common (introduced variety) • *Lotus corniculatus var. sativus*
Bird's-foot-trefoil, Common (native variety) • *Lotus corniculatus var. corniculatus*
Bistort, Amphibious • *Persicaria amphibia*
Bitter-cress, Hairy • *Cardamine hirsuta*
Bitter-cress, Wavy • *Cardamine flexuosa*
Bittersweet • *Solanum dulcamara*
Black-bindweed • *Fallopia convolvulus*
Black-grass • *Alopecurus myosuroides*
Black-poplar, Hybrid • *Populus x canadensis 'Robusta' (P. nigra x P. deltoides)*
Blackthorn • *Prunus spinosa*
Bluebell • *Hyacinthoides non-scripta*
Bluebell, Hybrid • *Hyacinthoides non-scripta x H. hispanica*
Bracken • *Pteridium aquilinum*
Bramble • *Rubus fruticosus agg.*
Bramble, Cut-leaved • *Rubus laciniatus*
Bramble, 'Himalayan Giant' • *Rubus armeniacus*
Brome, Barren • *Anisantha sterilis*
Brome, False • *Brachypodium sylvaticum*
Brooklime • *Veronica beccabunga*
Brookweed • *Samolus valerandi*
Bryony, Black • *Tamus communis*
Bryony, White • *Bryonia dioica*
Buckthorn • *Rhamnus cathartica*
Buckthorn, Alder • *Frangula alnus*
Bugle • *Ajuga reptans*
Bugloss • *Anchusa arvensis*
Bulrush • *Typha latifolia*
Bur-reed, Branched • *Sparganium erectum*
Burdock, Greater • *Arctium lappa*
Burdock, Lesser • *Arctium minus*
Burnet, Fodder • *Sanguisorba minor subsp. muricata*
Burnet, Salad • *Sanguisorba minor subsp. minor*
Burnet-saxifrage • *Pimpinella saxifraga*
Buttercup, Celery-leaved • *Ranunculus sceleratus*
Buttercup, Creeping • *Ranunculus repens*
Buttercup, Meadow • *Ranunculus acris*
Butterfly-bush • *Buddleja davidii*

Campion, Bladder • *Silene vulgaris subsp. vulgaris*
Campion, Hybrid • *Silene x hampeana (S. latifolia x S. dioica)*
Campion, Red • *Silene dioica*
Campion, Rose • *Lychnis coronaria*

Campion, White • *Silene latifolia*
Canary-grass, Bulbous • *Phalaris aquatica*
Canary-grass, Reed • *Phalaris arundinacea*
Candytuft, Wild • *Iberis amara*
Caraway • *Carum carvi*
Carrot, Wild • *Daucus carota subsp. carota*
Celandine, Greater • *Chelidonium majus*
Celandine, Lesser (bulbiliferous) • *Ranunculus ficaria subsp. bulbilifer*
Centaury, Common • *Centaurium erythraea*
Centaury, Lesser • *Centaurium pulchellum*
Charlock • *Sinapis arvensis*
Cherry, Bird • *Prunus padus*
Cherry, Wild • *Prunus avium*
Chervil, Rough • *Chaerophyllum temulum*
Chickweed, Common • *Stellaria media*
Cinquefoil, Creeping • *Potentilla reptans*
Cleavers • *Galium aparine*
Clover, Red • *Trifolium pratense*
Clover, White • *Trifolium repens*
Club-rush, Grey • *Schoenoplectus tabernaemontani*
Club-rush, Sea • *Bolboschoenus maritimus*
Cock's-foot • *Dactylis glomerata*
Colt's-foot • *Tussilago farfara*
Columbine • *Aquilegia vulgaris*
Comfrey, Common • *Symphytum officinale*
Comfrey, Rough • *Symphytum asperum*
Comfrey, Russian • *Symphytum x uplandicum (S. officinale x S. asperum)*
Comfrey, White • *Symphytum orientale*
Corydalis, Yellow • *Pseudofumaria lutea*
Cotoneaster, Himalayan • *Cotoneaster simonsii*
Couch, Common • *Elytrigia repens subsp. repens*
Cowslip • *Primula veris*
Crane's-bill, Cut-leaved • *Geranium dissectum*
Crane's-bill, Dove's-foot • *Geranium molle*
Crane's-bill, Small-flowered • *Geranium pusillum*
Cress, Hoary • *Lepidium draba*
Cress, Thale • *Arabidopsis thaliana*
Cuckooflower • *Cardamine pratensis*
Cudweed, Marsh • *Gnaphalium uliginosum*
Currant, Red • *Ribes rubrum*
Cypress, Leyland • *X Cupressocyparis leylandii*
  (Cupressus macrocarpa x Chamaecyparis nootkatensis)

Daffodil, Garden • *Narcissus pseudonarcissus cultivar*
Daisy • *Bellis perennis*

Daisy, Oxeye • *Leucanthemum vulgare*
Dame's-violet • *Hesperis matronalis*
Dandelion • *Taraxacum vulgare agg.*
Dead-nettle, Red • *Lamium purpureum*
Dead-nettle, Spotted • *Lamium maculatum*
Dead-nettle, White • *Lamium album*
Dewberry • *Rubus caesius*
Dock, Broad-leaved • *Rumex obtusifolius*
Dock, Clustered • *Rumex conglomeratus*
Dock, Curled • *Rumex crispus*
Dock, Fiddle • *Rumex pulcher*
Dock, Water • *Rumex hydrolapathum*
Dock, Wood • *Rumex sanguineus*
Dog's-tail, Crested • *Cynosurus cristatus*
Dog-rose • *Rosa canina*
Dog-rose, Hybrid (Dog-rose x Glaucous Dog-rose) • *Rosa x dumalis*
  (*R. canina x R. caesia subsp. glauca*)
Dogwood • *Cornus sanguinea*
Dogwood, White • *Cornus alba*
Duckweed, Common • *Lemna minor*
Duckweed, Least • *Lemna minuta*

Elder • *Sambucus nigra*
Elm, Small-leaved • *Ulmus minor subsp. minor*
Elm, Wych • *Ulmus glabra*
Enchanter's-nightshade • *Circaea lutetiana*
Evening-primrose, Large-flowered • *Oenothera glazioviana*

Fat-hen • *Chenopodium album*
Fern-grass • *Catapodium rigidum*
Fescue, Meadow • *Festuca pratensis*
Fescue, Rat's-tail • *Vulpia myuros*
Feverfew • *Tanacetum parthenium*
Field-speedwell, Common • *Veronica persica*
Field-speedwell, Grey • *Veronica polita*
Figwort, Water • *Scrophularia auriculata*
Figwort, Yellow • *Scrophularia vernalis*
Fleabane, Blue • *Erigeron acer*
Fleabane, Canadian • *Conyza canadensis*
Fleabane, Common • *Pulicaria dysenterica*
Fluellen, Round-leaved • *Kickxia spuria*
Forget-me-not, Early • *Myosotis ramosissima*
Forget-me-not, Field • *Myosotis arvensis*
Forget-me-not, Tufted • *Myosotis laxa subsp. caespitosa*
Forget-me-not, Water • *Myosotis scorpioides*

Forget-me-not, Wood • *Myosotis sylvatica*
Fox-sedge, False • *Carex otrubae*
Foxglove • *Digitalis purpurea*
Fumitory, Common (subspecies) • *Fumaria officinalis subsp. wirtgenii*
Fumitory, Few-flowered • *Fumaria vaillantii*

Gipsywort • *Lycopus europaeus*
Goat's-beard • *Tragopogon pratensis subsp. minor*
Goat's-rue • *Galega officinalis*
Goldenrod, Early • *Solidago gigantea subsp. serotina*
Goosefoot, Red • *Chenopodium rubrum*
Goosefoot, Swedish • *Chenopodium suecicum*
Ground-elder • *Aegopodium podagraria*
Ground-ivy • *Glechoma hederacea*
Groundsel • *Senecio vulgaris*
Groundsel, Sticky • *Senecio viscosus*
Guelder-rose • *Viburnum opulus*

Hart's-tongue • *Phyllitis scolopendrium*
Hawkbit, Autumn • *Leontodon autumnalis*
Hawkbit, Lesser • *Leontodon saxatilis*
Hawkbit, Rough • *Leontodon hispidus*
Hawk's-beard, Beaked • *Crepis vesicaria*
Hawk's-beard, Smooth • *Crepis capillaris*
Hawthorn • *Crataegus monogyna*
Hazel • *Corylus avellana*
Hedge-parsley, Upright • *Torilis japonica*
Hemlock • *Conium maculatum*
Hemp-agrimony • *Eupatorium cannabinum*
Herb-Robert • *Geranium robertianum*
Hogweed • *Heracleum sphondylium subsp. sphondylium*
Hogweed, Giant • *Heracleum mantegazzianum*
Holly • *Ilex aquifolium*
Honesty • *Lunaria annua*
Honeysuckle, Wilson's • *Lonicera nitida*
Hop • *Humulus lupulus*
Horehound, Black • *Ballota nigra subsp. meridionalis*
Hornbeam • *Carpinus betulus*
Horse-radish • *Armoracia rusticana*
Horsetail, Field • *Equisetum arvense*
Horsetail, Marsh • *Equisetum palustre*

Iris, Bearded cultivar • *Iris germanica group*
Iris, Stinking • *Iris foetidissima*
Iris, Yellow • *Iris pseudacorus*

Ivy • *Hedera helix*
Ivy, Persian • *Hedera colchica*

Knapweed, Common • *Centaurea nigra*
Knapweed, Greater • *Centaurea scabiosa*
Knotgrass • *Polygonum aviculare agg.*

Laburnum • *Laburnum anagyroides*
Lady's-mantle, Garden • *Alchemilla mollis*
Laurel, Cherry • *Prunus laurocerasus*
Lavender, Garden • *Lavandula x intermedia (L. angustifolia x L. latifolia)*
Lettuce, Prickly • *Lactuca serriola forma integrifolia*
Loosestrife, Yellow • *Lysimachia vulgaris*
Lords-and-Ladies • *Arum maculatum*
Lucerne • *Medicago sativa subsp. sativa*

Madder, Field • *Sherardia arvensis*
Male-fern • *Dryopteris filix-mas*
Mallow, Common • *Malva sylvestris*
Mallow, Dwarf • *Malva neglecta*
Maple, Field • *Acer campestre*
Mare's-tail • *Hippuris vulgaris*
Marjoram, Wild • *Origanum vulgare*
Marsh-marigold • *Caltha palustris*
Marsh-orchid, Southern • *Dactylorhiza praetermissa*
Mayweed, Scented • *Matricaria recutita*
Mayweed, Scentless • *Tripleurospermum inodorum*
Meadow-grass, Annual • *Poa annua*
Meadow-grass, Flattened • *Poa compressa*
Meadow-grass, Rough • *Poa trivialis*
Meadow-grass, Smooth • *Poa pratensis*
Meadowsweet • *Filipendula ulmaria*
Medick, Black • *Medicago lupulina*
Medick, Spotted • *Medicago arabica*
Melilot, Ribbed • *Melilotus officinalis*
Mercury, Annual • *Mercurialis annua*
Michaelmas-daisy, Common • *Aster x salignus (A. novi-belgii x A. lanceolatus)*
Mignonette, Wild • *Reseda lutea*
Mint, Corn • *Mentha arvensis*
Mint, Water • *Mentha aquatica*
Mint, Whorled • *Mentha x verticillata (M. arvensis x M. aquatica)*
Mouse-ear, Common • *Cerastium fontanum subsp. vulgare*
Mouse-ear, Sticky • *Cerastium glomeratum*
Mouse-ear-hawkweed • *Pilosella officinarum*
Mugwort • *Artemisia vulgaris*

Mullein, Dense-flowered • *Verbascum densiflorum*
Mullein, Great *Verbascum thapsus*
Mullein, Hybrid • *Verbascum x kerneri (V. phlomoides x V. thapsus)*
Mullein, Orange • *Verbascum phlomoides*
Mustard, Garlic • *Alliaria petiolata*
Mustard, Hedge • *Sisymbrium officinale*
Mustard, White • *Sinapis alba subsp. alba*

Narcissus cultivar • *Narcissus cultivar*
Nettle, Common • *Urtica dioica*
Nettle, Small • *Urtica urens*
Nettle, Stingless • *Urtica galeopsifolia*
Nightshade, Black • *Solanum nigrum subsp. nigrum*
Nightshade, Deadly • *Atropa belladonna*
Nipplewort • *Lapsana communis*
Nonea, Yellow • *Nonea lutea*

Oak, Pedunculate • *Quercus robur*
Oak, Red • *Quercus rubra*
Oat-grass, False • *Arrhenatherum elatius*
Oat-grass, Yellow • *Trisetum flavescens*
Orache, Common • *Atriplex patula*
Orchid, Bee • *Ophrys apifera*
Oregon-grape • *Mahonia aquifolium*
Osier • *Salix viminalis*
Oxtongue, Bristly • *Picris echioides*

Pansy, Field • *Viola arvensis*
Pansy, Garden • *Viola x wittrockiana*
Pansy, Wild • *Viola tricolor subsp. tricolor*
Parsley, Cow • *Anthriscus sylvestris*
Parsley, Fool's (dwarf subspecies) • *Aethusa cynapium subsp. agrestis*
Parsley, Fool's (type subspecies) • *Aethusa cynapium subsp. cynapium*
Parsley, Stone • *Sison amomum*
Parsley-piert • *Aphanes arvensis agg.*
Parsnip, Wild • *Pastinaca sativa var. sativa*
Pear, Wild • *Pyrus pyraster*
Pearlwort, Annual • *Sagina apetala*
Pearlwort, Procumbent • *Sagina procumbens*
Periwinkle, Greater • *Vinca major*
Persicaria, Pale • *Persicaria lapathifolia*
Pigmyweed, New Zealand • *Crassula helmsii*
Pimpernel, Scarlet • *Anagallis arvensis subsp. arvensis*
Pine, Scots • *Pinus sylvestris*
Pineappleweed • *Matricaria discoidea*

Pink-sorrel • *Oxalis articulata*
Plantain, Greater • *Plantago major*
Plantain, Ribwort • *Plantago lanceolata*
Plum, Wild • *Prunus domestica subsp. domestica*
Pond-sedge, Greater • *Carex riparia*
Pondweed, Broad-leaved • *Potamogeton natans*
Pondweed, Curled • *Potamogeton crispus*
Pondweed, Fennel • *Potamogeton pectinatus*
Poplar, Grey • *Populus x canescens (P. alba x P. tremula)*
Poppy, Common • *Papaver rhoeas*
Poppy, Opium • *Papaver somniferum subsp. somniferum*
Potato • *Solanum tuberosum*
Primrose • *Primula vulgaris*
Primula, Hybrid • *Primula veris x P. x polyantha*
Privet, Garden • *Ligustrum ovalifolium*
Privet, Wild • *Ligustrum vulgare*
Purple-loosestrife • *Lythrum salicaria*

Radish, Wild • *Raphanus raphanistrum subsp. raphanistrum*
Ragwort, Common • *Senecio jacobaea*
Ragwort, Hoary • *Senecio erucifolius*
Ragwort, Oxford • *Senecio squalidus*
Rape, Oil-seed • *Brassica napus subsp. oleifera*
Raspberry • *Rubus idaeus*
Redshank • *Persicaria maculosa*
Reed, Common • *Phragmites australis*
Rowan • *Sorbus aucuparia*
Rush, Hard • *Juncus inflexus*
Rush, Sharp-flowered • *Juncus acutiflorus*
Rush, Toad • *Juncus bufonius*
Rye-grass, Perennial • *Lolium perenne*

Sandwort, Slender • *Arenaria serpyllifolia subsp. leptoclados*
Sandwort, Thyme-leaved • *Arenaria serpyllifolia subsp. serpyllifolia*
Scabious, Field • *Knautia arvensis*
Scabious, Small • *Scabiosa columbaria*
Sedge, Glaucous • *Carex flacca*
Sedge, Hairy • *Carex hirta*
Selfheal • *Prunella vulgaris*
Shepherd's-needle • *Scandix pecten-veneris*
Shepherd's-purse • *Capsella bursa-pastoris*
Silverweed • *Potentilla anserina*
Small-reed, Wood • *Calamagrostis epigejos*
Snowberry • *Symphoricarpos albus*
Snowdrop • *Galanthus nivalis*

Snowdrop, Hybrid • *Galanthus nivalis x G. plicatus*
Soapwort (double-flowered) • *Saponaria officinalis flore pleno*
Soft-rush • *Juncus effusus*
Sorrel, Common • *Rumex acetosa*
Sow-thistle, *Perennial* • *Sonchus arvensis*
Sow-thistle, Prickly • *Sonchus asper*
Sow-thistle, Smooth • *Sonchus oleraceus*
Speedwell, Germander • *Veronica chamaedrys*
Speedwell, Ivy-leaved • *Veronica hederifolia*
Speedwell, Slender • *Veronica filiformis*
Speedwell, Thyme-leaved • *Veronica serpyllifolia*
Speedwell, Wall • *Veronica arvensis*
Spike-rush, Common • *Eleocharis palustris*
Spindle • *Euonymus europaeus*
Spotted-orchid, Common • *Dactylorhiza fuchsii*
Spotted-orchid, Common (?hybrid with Southern Marsh-orchid)
    • *Dactylorhiza ?x grandis (D. fuchsii x D. praetermissa)*
Spurge, Caper • *Euphorbia lathyris*
Spurge, Dwarf (cornfield subsp.) • *Euphorbia exigua subsp. segetalis*
Spurge, Petty • *Euphorbia peplus*
Spurge, Sun • *Euphorbia helioscopia*
St John's-wort, Perforate • *Hypericum perforatum*
St John's-wort, Square-stalked • *Hypericum tetrapterum*
Stonecrop, Biting • *Sedum acre*
Stonecrop, White • *Sedum album*
Stork's-bill, Common • *Erodium cicutarium*
Strawberry, Wild • *Fragaria vesca*
Sweet-briar • *Rosa rubiginosa*
Sweet-grass, Floating • *Glyceria fluitans*
Swine-cress • *Coronopus squamatus*
Swine-cress, Lesser • *Coronopus didymus*
Sycamore • *Acer pseudoplatanus*

Tansy • *Tanacetum vulgare*
Tare, Smooth • *Vicia tetrasperma*
Teaplant, Duke of Argyll's • *Lycium barbarum*
Teasel, Wild • *Dipsacus fullonum*
Thistle, Cotton • *Onopordum acanthium*
Thistle, Creeping • *Cirsium arvense*
Thistle, Marsh • *Cirsium palustre*
Thistle, Spear • *Cirsium vulgare*
Thistle, Welted • *Carduus crispus subsp. multiflorus*
Thyme, Wild • *Thymus polytrichus*
Timothy • *Phleum pratense*
Toadflax, Common • *Linaria vulgaris*

Toadflax, Ivy-leaved • *Cymbalaria muralis subsp. muralis*
Toadflax, Purple • *Linaria purpurea*
Traveller's-joy • *Clematis vitalba*
Treacle-mustard • *Erysimum cheiranthoides*
Trefoil, Hop • *Trifolium campestre*
Trefoil, Lesser • *Trifolium dubium*
Tulip, Garden • *Tulipa gesneriana*
Twayblade, Common • *Listera ovata*

Vervain • *Verbena officinalis*
Vetch, Common (ex-cultivation) • *Vicia sativa subsp. segetalis*
Vetch, Kidney • *Anthyllis vulneraria subsp. vulneraria*
Vetch, Tufted • *Vicia cracca*
Vetchling, Meadow • *Lathyrus pratensis*
Violet, Sweet • *Viola odorata*
Viper's-bugloss • *Echium vulgare*

Walnut • *Juglans regia*
Water-cress • *Rorippa nasturtium-aquaticum*
Water-crowfoot, Thread-leaved • *Ranunculus trichophyllus*
Water-plantain • *Alisma plantago-aquatica*
Water-plantain, Narrow-leaved • *Alisma lanceolatum*
Water-speedwell, Blue • *Veronica anagallis-aquatica*
Water-speedwell, Pink • *Veronica catenata*
Wayfaring-tree • *Viburnum lantana*
Weld • *Reseda luteola*
Whitlowgrass, Common • *Erophila verna*
Wild-oat • *Avena fatua*
Willow, Almond • *Salix triandra*
Willow, Crack • *Salix fragilis*
Willow, Goat • *Salix caprea subsp. caprea*
Willow, ?Green-leaved • *Salix ?x rubra (S. purpurea x S. viminalis)*
Willow, Grey (Rusty) • *Salix cinerea subsp. oleifolia*
Willow, Holme • *Salix x calodendron (S. viminalis x S. caprea x S. cinerea)*
Willow, Hybrid (Goat Willow x Grey Willow)
    • *Salix x reichardtii (S. caprea x S. cinerea)*
Willow, Purple • *Salix purpurea*
Willow, Weeping (Golden)
    • *Salix x sepulcralis nothovar. chrysocoma (S. alba x S. babylonica)*
Willow, White • *Salix alba*
Willowherb, American • *Epilobium ciliatum*
Willowherb, Great • *Epilobium hirsutum*
Willowherb, Hoary • *Epilobium parviflorum*
Willowherb, Rosebay • *Chamerion angustifolium*
Willowherb, Short-fruited • *Epilobium obscurum*

Willowherb, Square-stalked • *Epilobium tetragonum*
Winter-cress • *Barbarea vulgaris*
Woundwort, Hedge • *Stachys sylvatica*

Yarrow • *Achillea millefolium*
Yellow-cress, Creeping • *Rorippa sylvestris*
Yellow-cress, Great • *Rorippa amphibia*
Yellow-wort • *Blackstonia perfoliata*
Yew • *Taxus baccata*
Yorkshire-fog • *Holcus lanatus*

Appendix 4

GAME RECORDS

The annual game records illustrate how as the habitat improved over the first twelve years, so correspondingly did the total head of game from 63 to 1020. The average of 1046 for the last ten seasons shows that having created good habitat, consistently good results can be achieved even with amateur part-time keepering.

ANNUAL GAME TOTALS 1971 - 1993

	PHEASANTS	PARTRIDGES	WOODCOCK	SNIPE	DUCK	GEESE	HARES	RABBITS	PIGEONS	VARIOUS	
1971/72	24		16	6	8		1	8			63
1972/73	39		8	1	2			38	9	15	112
1973/74	108		12		1	2	2	55	1	4	185
1974/75	111		2	10	8		3	76	26	10	246
1975/76	118	5	8	10	42	7		113	47	22	372
1976/77	104		15	3	63	4		116	4	5	314
1977/78	111		13	3	28	6		135	40	9	345
1978/79	87		15	1	22			136	142	19	422
1979/80	135	32	12	4	26			45	79	24	357
1980/81	211	45	2		28	26		118	120	29	579
1981/82	194	31	7		81	2		115	263	19	722
1982/83	308		9	3	185			259	221	35	1020
1983/84	318		14	1	152	4		149	267	56	961
1984/85	306		17	5	73			254	214	27	896
1985/86	402		14	2	110	5		278	249	32	1092
1986/87	438		6		78	3	1	156	283	41	1006
1987/88	453		8		145	1		192	131	43	973
1988/89	481		6		151			37	154	29	858
1989/90	494		4		89	3		146	111	69	916
1990/91	438		6		82			174	164	22	888
1991/92	450		6		176	4		217	259	17	1129
1992/93	450		7		98	8		305	186	20	1074

Continuation of game records since WILL'S SHOOT was published in 1993

The eleven seasons show a continued consistency of overall sport and total

Game released has remained constant each season. 600 – 800 Pheasants
150 Mallard
1994 – 2000 – 100 French Partridges

	PHEASANTS	PARTRIDGES	WOODCOCK	SNIPE	DUCK	GEESE	HARES	RABBITS	PIGEONS	VARIOUS	
1993/94	576		3		149	13	4	46	145	19	955
1994/95	574	26	2		139	15	1	30	268	22	1 077
1995/96	504	21	9		147	11		80	103	14	891
1996/97	440	49	6		181	11		36	184	15	922
1997/98	456	23	4		184	4	2	161	140	21	995
1998/99	605	24	3		179	19		314	244	37	1 425
1999/2000	502	8	8		142	12	1	213	243	42	1 170
2000/01	591	5	2		172	1		119	116	37	1 043
2001/02	449		9		147	2		8	157	10	782
2002/03	564		8		149	6		144	121	26	1 018
2003/04	543		2		147	9		143	253	41	1 138

HAUXTON PITS SHOOT 2003/4

		PHEASANTS	PARTRIDGES	WOODCOCK	RABBITS	HARES	DUCK	GEESE	PIGEONS	VARIOUS	
6 NOV	7 GUNS	91					26		1	4	122
17 NOV	7 GUNS	105					13			4	122
27 NOV	7 GUNS	71		1			26	3	3	2	106
9 DEC	7 GUNS	73					34		4	2	113
18 DEC	8 GUNS	58					15		1		74
8 JAN	12 GUNS	36		1			15	5	87	1	145
15 JAN	5 GUNS	74					7		55	4	140
20 JAN	7 GUNS	29					7	1	17	4	58
29 JAN	5 GUNS	6					4		23	15	48
	OTHER				143				62	5	210
		543		2	143		147	9	253	41	1138

822 total for 7 driven days ∴ 117.4 average p. day

928 total for 7 driven + 2 marauds ∴ 103.1 average per day.

700 cock pheasant poults (french black-necks) 20 July
150 mallard
Pheasant returns of toe slit marked birds 402/700 = 57.4% + 3 from 2002
other pheasants shot, 90 cocks + 48 hens.
Total head of game stocked 850 - reared game shot 549 = 64.58%.
Comments : Fine hot, dry summer was good for reared game. French
black-necked pheasants held and flew v. well indeed. Best
breed of birds for Hauxton. Duck also flew well and guns
were limited as usual to 7 shots during a day. Non lead
cartridges used on all game days. Helpers day had a
bonus of v. good pigeon flight as did 15th Jan. A cool
drive boosted bag on 29 Jan.

A RECORD to produce over 100 head for the 9 days.
This inspite of reducing by 50 again the pheasant poults.
However we have a bonus of about 100 American x
pheasants from elsewhere.

The end of a successful drive on the helpers' day.